D0699242

Introducing Christian Ethics

Introducing

CHRISTIAN
ETHICS

Henlee H. Barnette

BROADMAN PRESS
Nashville, Tennessee

© 1961 · BROADMAN PRESS
Nashville, Tennessee
All rights reserved
International copyright secured

ISBN: 0–8054–6102–7
4261–02

Library of Congress catalog card number 61–5629
Printed in the United States of America

To Helen

Preface

Christian ethics has been a concern of the church through the centuries. Clement of Alexander (ca. A.D. 150–ca.213) was among the first Christian thinkers to deal with ethics per se in his work entitled *The Instructor*. Hence, he is recognized as the "first professor of Christian ethics." In succeeding generations such giants of the church as Augustine (354–430) in *Morals of the Catholic Church*, Thomas Aquinas (1224–1274) in *Summa Theologica*, John Calvin (1509–1564) in *Institutes of Religion*, and Walter Rauschenbusch (1861–1918) in *Christianizing the Social Order* had much to say in these and other works about ethics and moral philosophy.

As a distinctly separate discipline, Christian ethics, both Roman Catholic and Protestant, dates only from the Reformation. Philip Melanchthon (1497–1560) is accredited with having produced the first statement of Protestant ethics in his *Epitome of Moral Philosophy* (1538). Later, Schleiermacher (1768–1834) divided theology into two sections, dogmatics and ethics, giving the latter an independent treatment. Since this time, there has been a trend to treat Christian ethics as a separate and legitimate discipline.

Recent decades have witnessed a growing concern for the ethical aspects of the Christian faith both in Europe and America. In American theological seminaries during the past fifty years there has been a perceptible shift from the strictly traditional theological studies to those dealing with the relation of Christianity to social issues. An examination of eighty-seven American seminaries with membership in the American Association of Theological

Schools reveals that these institutions offer from two to sixty-eight hours in the general area of Christian ethics. Nine of these schools have departments devoted solely to Christianity and social problems.

During the past three decades a spate of books has been published in the area of social Christianity. Among the significant works on Protestant ethics to appear in this period are Emil Brunner's *The Divine Imperative* (1937, translated from the German edition of 1932); Reinhold Niebuhr's *An Interpretation of Christian Ethics* (1935); A. C. Knudson's *The Principles of Christian Ethics* (1948); Paul Ramsey's *Basic Christian Ethics* (1950); and George Thomas' *Christian Ethics and Moral Philosophy* (1957).

The purpose of this volume—and its justification—is to provide an introduction to Christian ethics which gives more attention to the biblical basis and the role of the Holy Spirit than is usually given in current texts on the subject. It is hoped that both college and seminary students who have had no orientation in Christian ethics will find the book helpful.

Part One of the study is concerned with the basic principles of Christian morality. The nature and scope of Christian ethics are discussed. Then the ethical content of the Old Testament is examined with attention given to the ethics of the law, the prophets, and the sages. The ethical teachings of Jesus, Paul, and other New Testament writers are considered, with particular attention given to the role of the Holy Spirit in morality.

Part Two is devoted to the problems of Christian ethics. Here, responsibility to self and to society is discussed. Suggestions as to the task of the church in relation to social issues appear in most chapters in this section.

Many minds go into the making of a book. It is impossible to acknowledge by name all persons who have directly or indirectly contributed to the making of this one. Every effort has been made to adequately document materials appropriated from many sources.

I am grateful to the trustees of the Southern Baptist Theological Seminary for giving me a sabbatical and to the Commission on Faculty Fellowships of the American Association of Theological Schools for awarding me a grant to study at Harvard University, during which time this volume was written.

Also, I wish to express my appreciation to Mrs. E. Glenn Hinson for typing both the rough draft and final copy of the manuscript.

Unless otherwise indicated, all Scripture references are taken from the Revised Standard Version of the Bible.

HENLEE H. BARNETTE

Contents

Part One
PRINCIPLES

I. Introduction   3
  1. What Is Christian Ethics?   3
  2. The Task and Scope of Christian Ethics 3
  3. Types of Christian Ethics   5
  4. Christian Ethics and Other Disciplines 6
  5. Why Study Christian Ethics?   9

II. Characteristics of Hebrew Morality   12
  1. Biblical Ground of Hebrew Ethics   12
  2. Ethical Limitations   16

III. Ethics of the Decalogue   19
  1. Duties to God   19
  2. Duties to Man   22
  3. Duty to Self   24

IV. Ethics of the Prophets   26
  1. The Prophet's Milieu   26
  2. The Prophet and His Role   27
  3. Presuppositions and Principles   28
  4. Problems of the Prophet   29
  5. The Contribution of the Prophets   33

V. Ethics of the Sages   35
  1. The Ethics of Job   36
  2. The Ethics of the Psalms   37
  3. The Ethics of Proverbs   37
  4. The Ethics of Ecclesiastes   40
  5. The Ethics of the Song of Songs   40

VI. Essential Character of Christ's Ethics   42
1. The Master Teacher of Morality 42
2. "Out of His Treasure Things Old and New" 43
3. "His Kingdom and His Righteousness" 46

VII. Content of Christ's Ethics   50
1. The Context of the Sermon 50
2. The Content of the Sermon 51
3. Summary and Conclusion 66

VIII. Ethics of Paul   69
1. Theological Bases 69
2. Ethical Principles 71
3. Incentives of Christian Behavior 73
4. Pauline Realism 76

IX. Ethics of Other New Testament Writers   79
1. The Johannine Corpus 79
2. Epistle to the Hebrews 81
3. Epistle of James 82
4. First Epistle of Peter 82
5. Second Epistle of Peter 84
6. Epistle of Jude 85

X. Ethics of the Holy Spirit   87
1. The Ethical Nature of the Holy Spirit 88
2. The Ethical Role of the Holy Spirit 89
3. The Holy Spirit and Contemporary Ethics 93

Part Two
PROBLEMS

XI. Duties to Self   101
1. Self-love Versus Selfless Love 101
2. The New Commandment and Agape-love 103
3. Some Specific Duties to Self 106

XII. Marriage and the Family   111
1. The Biblical Basis of Marriage 111
2. Divorce and Remarriage 113
3. The Christian View of Sex 117
4. Preparation for Marriage 119
5. Personality Interaction in the Family 120
6. The Church and the Family 125

XIII. **Race Relations** 128
1. The American Dilemma 128
2. The Problem of Prejudice 131
3. The Biblical Perspective of Racial Segregation . . . 135
4. The Role of the Church in the Reduction of Racial Tensions 139

XIV. **Economic Life** 144
1. The Biblical Perspective of Possessions 144
2. Christian Economic Concern Through the Centuries . . 148
3. The American Capitalistic Economy 152
4. The Christian Doctrine of Vocation 155
5. The Economic Problem in World Perspective . . . 157

XV. **Political Life** 161
1. The New Testament Attitude Toward the State . . . 161
2. The State: Its Nature and Function 164
3. Forms of the Modern State 166
4. Church-State Relations 168
5. The Problem of War and Peace 171
6. The Christian as a Citizen 172

Index 175

Part One: Principles

I

Introduction

What Is Christian Ethics?

Christian ethics is defined in a variety of ways by writers dealing with the subject. For instance, L. S. Keyser, American Lutheran scholar, defines this discipline as "the science which treats of the sources, principles, and practices of right and wrong in the light of the Holy Scriptures, in addition to the light of reason and nature." [1] Emil Brunner, Swiss theologian, declares that Christian ethics is "the science of human conduct as it is determined by Divine conduct." [2] Georgia Harkness, American Methodist theologian, conceives of Christian ethics as "a systematic study of the way of life exemplified and taught by Jesus, applied to the manifold problems and decisions of human existence." [3]

Since the above definitions are representative, they provide the student with some idea as to the general direction which studies in Christian ethics take. The approach taken in this volume gives more emphasis to the role of the Spirit in moral action than is usually the case. Christian ethics, therefore, is defined as a systematic explanation of the moral example and teaching of Jesus applied to the total life of the individual in society and actualized by the power of the Spirit. The remainder of this study is an effort to elaborate this operational definition into a systematic statement of Christian ethics.

The Task and Scope of Christian Ethics

Ethics has a twofold function, first, to define the "Highest Good," and second, to declare the principles of human action

3

necessary to achieve this goal. In philosophical ethics, the search for the *summum bonum* of life has led to numerous theories such as pleasure, happiness, power, duty for duty's sake, and self-realization.[4] In contrast to philosophical ethics, biblical revelation sets forth the will of God as the ethical goal of man. By means of biblical exegesis and interpretation, the Christian ethicist seeks to determine the nature and purpose of God's will for human action. He must define those basic norms of revelation by which man may act in keeping with the will of God. To make these norms relevant to contemporary moral decisions, the insights of philosophy, history, and the social sciences may be utilized. Hence, Christian ethics is bifocal, looking to the Bible for the norms or principles of behavior and to other disciplines for factual data for intelligent action.

As for the scope of Christian ethics, differences of opinion prevail among evangelical Christians. Some tend to narrow the sphere of Christian ethics to the individual, excluding the society in which he lives. Others become so concerned with the problems of the social order that they tend to neglect the spiritual needs of the individual. Hence, Christianity is ethicized or reduced to a social program. This was the error of left-wing American liberal theology in which the kingdom of God tended to become identified with the perfectibility of man and social progress.

There is no such thing as a "personal" gospel as over against a "social" gospel. There is but one gospel which is both personal and social. Personal regeneration and social reconstruction are demanded by the gospel. The redeemed man must seek the redemption of the society in which he lives. He is the salt of the earth and the light of the world. The areas of marriage, industry, and state are, as is the individual, under the judgment of God. The Christian, therefore, is called not merely to live in these areas, but to do his part in bringing them more in accord with the will and purpose of God.

Adiaphorism is related to the problem of the scope of Christian ethics. Since certain actions appear to be neither good nor bad, they are classified as adiaphora, the morally neutral. Situations do arise in which the question of wrong choice does not appear, but even then a decision is made in terms of what is generally accepted as right. Even in this kind of a situation one remains morally responsible, because the will of God applies to the total life of the Christian and at every moment of his existence.

Types of Christian Ethics

In Christian history various types of ethics have been developed. They may be differentiated broadly on the basis of religious groups: early Church, Catholic—Roman and Greek Orthodox, and Protestant. Again, they may be classified in terms of social outlook: Monasticism, theocracy, legalism, pietism, liberalism, and religious socialism. Or they may be distinguished by their integrating concepts: natural law, love, the kingdom of God, the Incarnation, the Trinity, the idea of perfection, the imitation of Christ, the vision of God, the new being, the idea of happiness or well-being.[5] Each of these integrating concepts may be interpreted in a variety of ways. Christian love, for example, may mean both self-love and selfless love; wholly selfless love; the bifurcation of love into sacrificial and mutual love; solely neighbor love and/or community love.

Christian ethics is classified broadly in terms of teleological and deontological ethics. Teleological ethics begins with the problem of the goal or end of man. Under this category the vision of God,[6] human perfection,[7] and the kingdom of God,[8] are posited as the ethical goals of man.

Deontological ethics is an ethics of obedience. Theologians who follow this method are more concerned with the demand of God than the goal of man in ethics. It is an ethics of radical obedience to the will of God. Those who take the deontological position may be divided into two broad categories: biblical literalists and formal ethicists. The former conceive of morality in terms of obedience to the letter of the law, making the Bible a code book of ethics. The latter tend to reduce the revealed ethical commands to the love of God and neighbor to which God demands radical obedience.[9]

It should be obvious that Christian ethics is both deontological and teleological in nature. The former is illustrated in Jesus'

Gethsemane prayer: "Thy will be done"; the latter is stated in his model prayer: "Thy kingdom come." As L. H. Marshall declares: "The ethics of Jesus can be classified neither as the 'Ethics of Duty' nor as the 'Ethics of Ends,' for it is a combination of the two, 'Duty' being represented by the will of God, and the 'End' as the realization of the Kingdom of God." [10]

Contemporary Protestant ethics may be classified into several "families" with conversations going on between them. Among these families are the liberals, fundamentalists, "neo-orthodox," Christian actionists, and Anglicans. The ethics of liberalism is expressed in the so-called "Social Gospel" with an elaboration of the kingdom of God as a social reality on earth. Due to a rigid literalism fundamentalist ethics is legalistic, viewing morality as conformity to codes and rules of conduct. In general, the "neo-orthodox" and Christian actionist groups lay emphasis upon love as relevant in person-to-person relations but largely irrelevant in society since love tends to break down in the "collective brutalities" of the social order. Hence, exponents of these groups derive rationalistic principles in terms of "middle-axioms" (more concrete principles to mediate between the universal principle of love and the social structures) which are applied to the social order.[11] Anglican (English) ethics is an ethics of natural law based upon the theory that Christian morality is the highest version of natural morality written in nature and in rational man.[12]

While there is some overlapping in the above "families" of Christian ethics, they do fall into the broad types described. And though brief and incomplete, this discussion provides the student with some notion as to the complexity of Christian ethics and the types elaborated by contemporary theologians. With the passage of time, we may expect other emphases to emerge as the search goes on for a realistic ethic for the atomic and space age.

Christian Ethics and Other Disciplines

Christian ethics and theology are organically and inseparably related. God is the ground of all Christian morality. Thus, ethics and theology can be separated only for purposes of study and focus of interest. When divorced from its theological ground, the

Christian ethic becomes nothing more than a humanistic ideal. An intimate relation also exists between Christian ethics and the various branches of theology. For instance, Christian ethics co-operates with biblical studies in setting out the ethical content of the Bible; with church history by surveying the ethical emphases of the church through the centuries; with homiletics in proclaiming social concern; with pastoral counseling to reduce anxieties and frustrations by getting at the moral sense of guilt; with missions in preparing men to meet ethical issues on mission fields; and with religious education by inculcating and implementing ethical truth.

Christian ethics is fundamentally related to psychology, the science of the mind and human behavior. Man's moral faculties are a basic part of his mental constitution. Questions essential to moral action such as character, conscience, and will, involve states of the acting individual's mind. No adequate judgment can be made of an act, right or wrong, good or bad, until the motive which lies at the root of all conduct is known.

Contemporary psychiatrists and psychologists are becoming aware of the vital connection between psychology and ethics. Erich Fromm, eminent psychiatrist, has discovered that "Neurosis itself is, in the last analysis, a symptom of moral failure." [13] Psychologist Gordon Allport of Harvard says, "Most of the conflicts that cause damage to mental health . . . have to do with courses of conduct the individual regards as impulsively desirable and those he regards as morally obligatory. Whether we call it conscience or super-ego, the moral sense is most always involved in any serious conflict." [14]

Ethics, then, is related not only to correctness of conduct, the motives which actuate and determine it but also to the moral failure of the acting subject. Therefore, ethics and psychology stand in need of each other to understand man more fully.

Christian ethics has a vital relation to the various social sciences, particularly sociology. Ethics looks to these disciplines for data concerning social phenomena and for trustworthy knowledge of social conditions in which persons live. In other words, ethics turns to the social sciences for "what is" data and to the norms of biblical revelation for "what ought to be" data, bringing them into a coherent and relevant principle.

Finally, Christian ethics is related to philosophy. Both are concerned with the ultimate basis of conduct, the nature of right and wrong, values, epistemology, duty, happiness, man and society. Christian ethics thus may make use of philosophical insights which contribute to an understanding of these problems. However, Christian ethics must guard against shifting over "to the ground of rational moral Law." [15] Revised and transformed to be consistent with faith and love, certain philosophical ideas may be advantageous. Thus a "coalition" may be formed with any school of ethics grounded in philosophical insight, providing Christian love "always occupies the ground floor." [16]

A classical example of how love may use the insights of philosophical morality is seen in Augustine, one of the Fathers of the Church. [17] He defines the four "cardinal virtues" of the Greeks —wisdom, temperance, courage, and justice—in terms of love. In his thought, love is the essence of all virtue. Therefore, he reinterprets the Greek ideals as expressions of the principle of Christian love. Wisdom becomes love discerning aright what helps or hinders it toward God. Courage appears as love, readily bearing all things for the sake of the loved object. Justice appears as love serving God only, and therefore ruling well all else, as subject to man. Temperance turns out to be love, keeping itself entire and incorrupt for God. Admittedly, Neo-Platonic influence is manifested in this scheme, but it is Neo-Platonism thoroughly transformed and Christianized.

Even before the day of Augustine, the apostle Paul reflects the influence of the Greek moralists, especially the Stoics. For instance, he urges Christians to practice kindness and temperance (2 Cor. 6:6; Gal. 5:23; Titus 2:2), both of which are Greek ideas. Paul takes these ethical principles and transforms them, giving them a deeper meaning. [18] Yet, in Paul the Christian ethic remains unique, losing none of its real character. Love continues to be central in his ethical thought.

Obviously, a complete synthesis of Christian and philosophical morality is impossible, due to the transcendent nature of the

Christian ethic. Christian ethics begins with revelation while philosophical ethics starts with reason; the former possesses the truth while the latter pursues the truth. William Temple aptly summarizes the basic connection between rationalistic philosophy and biblical revelation when he says:

. . . all that philosophy could ever do would be to provide an intellectual introduction to religion. It could never supply religious faith itself. And let us also remember that there is this permanent ground of tension between religion and philosophy: that what are for philosophy the ultimate questions are for religion the primary assurances.[19]

Such high claims for Christianity lead the theologian and philosopher to eye each other with suspicion. To the theologian, the philosopher sometimes becomes a "secular play-boy in holy matters," while the theologian becomes an "arrogant dogmatist" to the philosopher.[20]

Christian ethicists may profitably appropriate, transform, and use the valid insights of the philosophical moralists, provided the distinctiveness of the Christian ethic is not sullied or lost. The Christian ethic must never lose its transmoral nature by excessive amalgamation with or accommodation to philosophical ideas. It must always remain more than just another splendid ethical teaching along with those of Plato, Seneca, Aristotle, and Kant.

Why Study Christian Ethics?

Among the most obvious reasons for a serious study of Christian ethics is that the Christian needs the light which it throws upon his own daily problems. Constantly he is forced to make moral decisions in complex and ambiguous situations. Hence, he needs all the ethical insight possible in the moral struggle.

It is especially imperative that ministers understand ethics in order to give sound moral guidance to their parishioners. Both those in and those out of the church need specific and sympathetic counsel with respect to the baffling problems which confront them. It is the task of the minister to furnish such counsel.

Again, the Christian needs an understanding of ethics to avoid common errors of ethical reasoning. Among these are: the error of reducing Christian morality to a mere set of rules; the error of permitting self interest to deflect moral judgment; the error of stressing minor ethical issues and neglecting major ones; the error of divorcing religion from ethics; and the fallacy of substituting ethical contemplation for ethical conduct.

Another reason for studying Christian ethics is that it stimulates one's own moral growth. Ethics provides a standard by which one can measure his own moral development. In the light of this standard the individual may see what he ought to be in terms of what he actually is. This creates a tension and a discontent, driving him toward the goal of perfection which God demands of his children.

Finally, the Christian should study Christian ethics because Jesus' teaching is ethical as well as theological. Therefore, no one can be an adequate interpreter of Christianity unless he understands and emphasizes the ethical content of the gospel.

References

1. Leander S. Keyser, *A Manual of Christian Ethics* (Burlington, Iowa: Lutheran Literary Board, 1926), p. 10; see chapter 1 for a list of definitions current a few decades ago.

2. Emil Brunner, *The Divine Imperative* (Philadelphia: Westminster Press, 1947), p. 86.

3. Georgia Harkness, *Christian Ethics* (New York: Abingdon Press, 1957), p. 15.

4. See R. A. Tsanoff, *The Moral Ideals of Our Civilization* (New York: E. P. Dutton & Co., 1942).

5. For a discussion of some of these motifs see Daniel Day Williams, *What Present-day Theologians Are Thinking* (New York: Harper & Bros., 1952), III.

6. K. E. Kirk, *The Vision of God: The Christian Doctrine of the Summum Bonum* (London: Longmans, Green & Co., 1931).

7. R. Newton Flew, *The Idea of Perfection in Christian Theology: An Historical Study of the Christian Ideal for the Present Life* (London: Oxford University Press, 1934).

8. Walter Rauschenbusch, *A Theology for the Social Gospel* (New York: Macmillan Co., 1917).

9. See Brunner, *op. cit.,* Part I.

10. L. H. Marshall, *The Challenge of New Testament Ethics* (New York: Macmillan Co., 1948), pp. 8–9.

11. John C. Bennett, *Christian Ethics and Social Policy* (New York: Charles Scribner's Sons, 1946), pp. 77–83.

12. H. H. Henson, *Christian Morality: Natural, Developing, Final* (London: Oxford at the Clarendon Press, 1936).

13. Erich Fromm, *Man for Himself* (New York: Rinehart & Co., 1947), p. viii.

14. G. W. Allport, *The Individual and His Religion: A Psychological Interpretation* (New York: Macmillan Co., 1950), p. 86.

15. Paul Ramsey, *Basic Christian Ethics* (New York: Charles Scribner's Sons, 1950), p. 340.

16. *Ibid.,* p. 344.

17. Philip Schaff (ed.), *Nicene and Post-Nicene Fathers,* "On the Morals of the Catholic Church," 15 (Buffalo: The Christian Literary Society, 1887), IV, 48.

18. J. B. Lightfoot, "St. Paul and Seneca," *Saint Paul's Epistle to the Philippians* (London: Macmillan Co., 1891), pp. 287 f.

19. W. Temple, *Basic Convictions* (New York: Harper & Bros., 1936), p. 1.

20. Virgilius Ferm, "Theology," *Encyclopedia of Religion* (New York: Philosophical Library, 1945), p. 782.

Recommended Reading

BRUNNER, EMIL, *The Divine Imperative.* Philadelphia: Westminster Press, 1947, "The Definition of Christian Ethics," IX.

"Ethics," *Encyclopedia of Religion and Ethics,* ed. JAMES HASTINGS, Vol. V, New York: Charles Scribner's Sons, 1912.

HARKNESS, GEORGIA, *Christian Ethics.* New York: Abingdon Press, 1957, Chapter I, "What Is Christian Ethics?"

THOMAS, GEORGE F., *Christian Ethics and Moral Philosophy.* New York: Charles Scribner's Sons, 1955, Chapter 17.

WHEELWRIGHT, PHILLIP, *A Critical Introduction to Ethics.* New York: Odyssey Press, 1949.

II

Characteristics of Hebrew Morality

A fundamental continuity prevails between Old and New Testament teaching. Hence, an understanding of Hebrew ethics is essential to an adequate knowledge of the ethics of Jesus and the New Testament as a whole. Christian ethics, therefore, requires an analysis of the characteristics and content of the main streams of morality in the Old Covenant.

Biblical Ground of Hebrew Ethics

Hebrew ethics is radically theocentric, being grounded in the Hebrew concept of the nature of God himself. God is the one creator, sovereign ruler, and Father (Deut. 6:4; Isa. 40:28; Mal. 2:10). In contrast to idols, "The Lord is the true God; he is the living God and the everlasting King" (Jer. 10:10). He is a Person, not a static "Being," who participates in history and human life. God is holy and requires holiness of his people: "you shall be holy; for I the Lord your God am holy" (Lev. 11:45; 19:2). God is righteous and demands righteousness of his children (Isa. 45:21; Amos 5:24).

Fellowship with God is inseparable from the good life: "He has showed you, O man, what is good; and what does the Lord require of you but to do justice, and to love kindness, and to walk humbly with your God?" (Mic. 6:8). Here ethics is inseparably related to personal fellowship with the living God.

Obedience to God's will is the basic principle of Old Testament ethics. As W. S. Bruce says, "The personal, living God is set forth as the ground of morals and all good is absolutely referred to His will." [1] It is "an unconditional obligation" to the will of God as the basis of character and conduct.[2] Thus, absolute obedience to the will of God is the highest good; disobedience is sin, a transgression of the law.

The content of the will of God is love (*'ahebh* and its derivatives). Basically, love is a personal feeling and force which involves fear (reverence) of God and a recognition and care of one's fellow man (both neighbor and enemy) as seen in Deuteronomy 6:5; 10:12; Leviticus 19:18,34. Love is never strictly a law, but the basis of all legal and social relationships. Thus, contrary to the popular notion, love plays a significant role in Hebrew ethics. It is this "dominant position" given to the idea of love that constitutes "the great glory of the Old Testament." [3]

In the Old Testament both election and covenant are based on the love of God. God chose Israel "for his own possession, out of all the peoples that are on the face of the earth" (Deut. 7:6). Why was Israel chosen above all other nations? Certainly she was not selected for her goodness and greatness (Deut. 7:7; 9:4–5). Rather, God's choice was motivated solely by unmerited love: "The Lord loves you, and is keeping the oath which he swore to your fathers, that the Lord has brought you out with a mighty hand, and redeemed you from the house of bondage, from the hand of Pharaoh king of Egypt" (Deut. 7:8).

God's love is also the ground of the covenant relation between himself and the Hebrews. As Norman Snaith has shown, love is "the cause" of the covenant and loyalty (*chesed*) to God its means of continuance.[4] This covenant-love relationship is more than a "mere bargain" for it implies, on the one hand, God's grace and deliverance, and on the other Israel's grateful obedience (see covenants Gen. 12:1 ff.; Ex. 20:1 ff.; 24:3–9; Deut. 4:13; 5:2; 9:9). There is, therefore, as H. H. Rowley says, "an ethical strand in the very establishment of the religion of Israel through Moses, since gratitude is essentially an ethical emotion." [5]

Both covenant and election-love involved moral responsibility and service. Israel was to respond to covenant-love with a personal, spontaneous, and sacrificial spirit (Lev. 19:18,34; Deut. 6:5). In this spirit she was to love God and keep his commandments (Ex. 20:1 ff.; Deut. 11:22; 19:9; 30:16). She was not only to love her neighbors but also her enemies (Lev. 19:18; Deut. 22:1–4; Ex. 23:4 f.). The concept of love in the Old Testament reached its consummation in God's suffering love as revealed in the book of Hosea.

God's election-love also included moral responsibility. Israel sometimes presumed that election would automatically guarantee God's presence and blessing. At the same time that the prophets were pronouncing God's judgment upon Israel's faithlessness, the nation's leaders were claiming: "Is not the Lord in the midst of us? No evil shall come upon us" (Mic. 3:11; Jer. 5:12). The prophet Amos sternly counseled that the nation was not to be so blinded by election as to forget her religious and moral duties (Amos 9:7–8). Against this sin God warned: "You only have I known of all the families of the earth; therefore I will punish you for all your iniquities" (Amos 3:2).

Divine election also involved service to God. Instead of a special privilege, it was election to participation in the purpose of God in the world. For, in the election, Israel became the property of God, a "kingdom of priests," a "holy nation" to perform a unique service. She was to be God's instrument for the redemption of man. Isaiah poetically described Israel's election-mission:

I have called you in righteousness,
I have taken you by the hand and kept you;
I have given you as a covenant to the people,
    a light to the nations,
to open the eyes that are blind,
to bring out the prisoners from the dungeon,
from the prison those who sit in darkness (Isa. 42:6–7).

The agent of God's will is man. While there is no uniform doctrine of anthropology in the Old Testament, the main elements are there. Man is a creature made in the image of God (Gen. 1:27). The meaning of the "image of God" as related to man is a subject of much controversy among the theologians. But two dominant ideas appear to be included; namely, the dignity and dominion of man.

Man's dignity is seen in the fact that he was made for fellowship with God. His distinctive quality, therefore, consists in the fact that God addresses man as person to person and that man has the capacity to answer. Man is able to hear God and to respond in faith to God's Word. Thus man is a responsible being before God.

The quality of dominion in man is seen in the fact that he shares in the sovereignty of God in the earth. The Hebrew term "image" always denotes a tangible representation in Semitic thought. Man, then, is God's representative in the world, sharing in his sovereignty (Gen. 1:27 ff.). That God has delegated a part of his sovereignty to man is clearly described by the Psalmist:

> What is man that thou art mindful of him,
>   and the son of man that thou dost care for him?
> Yet thou hast made him little less than God,
>   and dost crown him with glory and honor.
> Thou hast given him dominion over the works of
>   thy hands;
>   thou hast put all things under his feet (Psalm 8:4–6).

But man desired to be God and the supreme sovereign of all life. The creature aspired to be the Creator. Man's pride and disobedience resulted in the "Fall." Though the image of God in man was not lost in the "Fall" (Gen. 5:1–3; 9:5–6), it left man with a corrupt and wicked heart (Gen. 8:21). God alone can deliver man from his sinful predicament (Isa. 45:22; Jer. 8:7; 31:10).

Hebrew ethics also envisions a realistic view of sin. At least a dozen words are used in the Old Testament to describe sin in its various manifestations. One group denotes "missing the mark" (cf. Prov. 8:36); another group conveys a sense of "guilt" (Gen. 4:13; Psalm 38:4); another that of "vice" (1 Kings 16:25). Most dominant, however, is the idea of sin as "rebellion" against God (Amos 1:3 ff.; Mic. 1:5). Of course, sin is also a violation of the Law and the covenantal-brotherhood. Primarily, however, sin is against God himself. The psalmist points up this fact: "Against thee, thee only, have I sinned, and done that which is evil in thy sight" (Psalm 51:4). Sin is ultimately against God, not an ethical code or the customs of the community.

Old Testament ethics has as its social goal the realization of a universal kingdom of God. This kingdom has political connotations of national restoration of the Davidic kingdom in greater splendor and freedom. The coming of this kingdom is tied in with the advent of the Messiah-King, the Son of David, to whom will be given the sovereignty of God. One "like a son of man" receives the kingdom of God (Dan. 7:13). This future kingdom is to be characterized by an eternal reign of peace and righteousness. Even nature will be renovated, and both man and beast will dwell in happy harmony (Isa. 11:1–10).

Ethical Limitations

Hebrew ethics is widely accepted today as higher than that of ancient Israel's contemporaries. Yet her morality betrays several limitations. For example, Old Testament ethics is incomplete. It is an ethics for a people at an early stage of religious development. Hebrew ethics, therefore, finds its fulfilment in the higher ethics of Christ "in whom it blossomed into perfection." [6] As the religion of Israel finds full fruition in the Christian faith, so does her ethics. Hence, Hebrew ethics is not static but always developing toward the perfect morality of Jesus Christ.

Also, Old Testament ethics suffers from a dualism in its application. Though justice is a strong ethical demand in the Old Testament, it is not equally shared. For instance, a double-standard of justice prevails for the Hebrew and the foreigner. Usury among Hebrews is forbidden, but the Hebrew could loan money for interest to the foreigner (Deut. 23:19–20). Even within the Hebrew tribal circle certain individuals are denied full personal rights. In the case of women, for example, there is a tendency to assign her an inferior status in society. It is true that certain passages describe some women in a somewhat favorable light. At religious festivals a female could share in the demonstrations

(Deut. 12:12; Judg. 21:21). She could participate in some phases of the sanctuary activities (Ex. 38:8). And daughters could inherit a father's property provided there was no son (Num. 27:8). Certain women rise to prominent positions as judges or prophetesses (Ex. 15:20; Judg. 4:4; 2 Chron. 34:22 ff.). But, on the whole, women occupy a subordinate place in the community.

Treatment of slaves by the Hebrews was a great deal more humane than was the practice among their contemporaries. Most slaves were foreigners, purchased or taken in war (Gen. 17:12; Num. 31:11). Hebrews themselves became slaves as a result of stealing or debt, and possibly voluntarily to escape poverty (Ex. 21:7 ff.; Amos 2:6). Emancipation for the Hebrew slave was possible after six years of slavery (Ex. 21:2). Only death terminated the servitude of the foreign slave (Lev. 25:44–46). All Hebrew slaves, regardless of date of enslavement, were set free in the year of Jubilee which occurred every forty-nine years (Lev. 25:8).

Another characteristic of Old Testament ethics is the tendency toward legalism. Moral demands are interpreted in external terms of custom and ritual, while concern for motives and attitudes is largely absent from the ethical picture. In spite of the fact that the prophets laid down basic principles of righteousness, Israel developed a thoroughly legalistic approach to conduct after the Exile. By the time of Jesus, legalism was at its highest stage of development in Israel.

Some practices of the ancient Hebrews shock the Christian conscience. There was, for example, the practice of *cherem* in which an enemy city was devoted to Yahweh. In its extreme form, men, women, children, babies, cattle, and even inanimate objects were utterly destroyed (Deut. 13:16–18). *Cherem* of this nature was pronounced upon the Amalekites (Ex. 17:14; Deut. 25:19; 1 Sam. 15:3). Why did God command such savage destruction?

Two traditional answers have been presented for the justification of *cherem*. First, it was designed to prevent the Israelites from amalgamating with the Canaanites and consequently being lost as a nation; and second, it was a manifestation of God's judgment against the wicked Canaanites even as the Assyrians were his agents to punish Israel later (Isa. 10:5–6). Two additional observations may be made. The practice of *cherem* began to cease as early as the reign of David who spared the Jebusites when he took Jerusalem; and in the Old Testament, revelation was progressively apprehended by the Hebrews, and the measure of revelation for any period of Hebrew history was sufficient for that era. As the Hebrews advanced in their knowledge of God there was *pari passu*, progress in Hebrew morality. As J. M. Powis Smith concludes: "Ethics and theology advanced together, each supporting the other." [7] Therefore, we cannot fairly judge the ancient Hebrews by our Christian standards which they did not possess.

References

1. W. S. Bruce, *The Ethics of the Old Testament* (Edinburgh: T. & T. Clark, 1909), p. 16.

2. Walther Eichrodt, *Man in the Old Testament* (Chicago: Henry Regnery Co., 1951), p. 9.

3. See "Love," by Gottfried Quell and Ethelbert Stauffer, J. R. Coates (trans.), *Bible Key Words from Gehard Kittel's Theologisches Wöterbuch Zum Neuen Testament* (New York: Harper & Bros., 1951), p. 6; and Norman H. Snaith, *The Distinctive Ideas of the Old Testament* (London: Epworth Press, 1944), Chapters 5–6.

4. Snaith, *op. cit.*, p. 119.

5. H. H. Rowley, *Moses and the Decalogue* (Manchester: Manchester University Press, 1951), p. 101.

6. Bruce, *op. cit.*, p. 2.

7. J. Smith, *The Moral Life of the Hebrews* (Chicago: University Press, 1923), p. vii.

Recommended Reading

BRUCE, W. S., *The Ethics of the Old Testament*. Edinburgh: T. & T. Clark, 1909.

MITCHELL, H. G., *The Ethics of the Old Testament*. Chicago: The University Press, 1912.

SNAITH, NORMAN H., *The Distinctive Ideas of the Old Testament*. London: Epworth Press, 1944.

III

Ethics of the Decalogue

Central in the moral life of Israel are the Ten Commandments. Andrew Osborn has aptly observed: "The Ten Commandments are the cornerstone of Hebrew ethics, standing in the same relation to the religion of Israel as the Sermon on the Mount does to Christianity." [1] In this study we are primarily concerned with the "ethical" or "moral" Decalogue in Exodus 20:1–17.[2] This particular Decalogue is called "ethical" because "it is so much wider in its ethical demands than might be expected merely in view of the social conditions of the time, and because it penetrates beneath action to its spring in motive." [3]

The laws of the Decalogue are more than a mere collection of customs common to the contemporaries of the Hebrews. These moral injunctions are the commands of God, not the folkways and mores of the people (Ex. 20:1–2). They constitute, therefore, eternal, universal values indispensable for the fulfilment of the individual and society. Man's duty to God is summed up in the first four laws; the remaining six apply to man's duties to others and himself. In this chapter we shall attempt to set forth the basic moral principles embodied in each of these ten laws.

Duties to God

Commandment one.—"You shall have no other gods before me" (Ex. 20:3). This first commandment articulates the principle of the sovereignty of God. Since Yahweh alone is the God of Israel, there can be no others. He permits no divided loyalty on the part of his people. Later the cult of Baal, god of rain and fertility, was introduced as an addition to the religion of the He-

19

brews. The inevitable result was religious syncretism in which Yahweh was reduced to the level of the pagan gods. Elijah, the prophet, vigorously protested this religious amalgam in the contest between Baal and Yahweh on Mount Carmel (1 Kings 18:20–40).

Commandment two.—"You shall not make yourself a graven image . . ." (Ex. 20:4). This law requires purity of worship. The sovereign God is also spiritual and must be worshiped in spirit and truth. The Creator is not to be worshiped in the form of the creature. Material likenesses tend to turn the worshiper from the spirituality of God to the worship of the objects themselves. An excellent example of this tendency is seen in Hebrew history. King Hezekiah ordered the Nehushtan, the brazen serpent, destroyed because it had been perverted from a memorial relic into an idol (2 Kings 18:4).

God is jealous for the purity of worship, "visiting the iniquity of the fathers upon the children to the third and fourth generation" of them that hate him. It is a fact of experience that the consequences of a bad influence (not the guilt) of parents are visited upon their children. God's love, however, extends to thousands of generations which love him and keep his commandments.

Symbols and images of God are used almost universally by the churches today, especially by Roman and Eastern Orthodox Catholics. It is claimed that these objects are used merely as guides to worship. As long as one does not "bow down to them and serve them," it is argued, there is no violation of the commandment. But as this law implies and experience teaches, there is the constant danger of substituting the dead object for the living God.

Commandment three.—"You shall not take the name of the Lord your God in vain . . ." (Ex. 20:7). God's "name" as used in the Bible denotes his nature and personality (cf. Ex. 3:14). Embodied in this law is the principle of reverence for God in all deeds and words. Unfortunately this injunction has come to be associated primarily with profanity. Hebrew thought and language do not bear out this particularized interpretation. The term translated "take" (in the Hebrew, *nasa'*) means "to take up," "to carry," never to utter God's name (cf. Ex. 12:34; 25:14; 37:14). Thus, this commandment refers to an attitude of the heart, not an action of the tongue. God's name is never to be carried in vain or a false manner. To do this is to discredit his nature and person.

By implication the third commandment also forbids the misuse of God's name in any fashion. It prohibits perjury, that is, the use of God's name to attest to what is untrue (Lev. 19:12). Tangentially, it also forbids the use of profanity. Any word or deed which sullies the holy name of God is reprehensible: "The Lord will not hold him guiltless."

Commandment four.—"Remember the sabbath day, to keep it holy" (Ex. 20:8). The word translated "sabbath" comes from the Hebrew term *shabbath* meaning "to rest." God created all things in six days and rested on the seventh, blessing and sanctifying it. Hence, the sabbath appears to be a pre-Mosaic institution. It became a sign of covenant between God and his people (Ezek. 20:12). Also it became a day of thanksgiving for deliverance from Egypt (Lev. 19:34; Deut. 5:15), a weekly reminder of the Passover, just as, for the Christian, Sunday became a weekly reminder of the resurrection.

The Hebrew sabbath was both a day of rest and worship. Man and beast ceased their work on this day (Deut. 5:13–15). Both needed the restoring influence of a day of rest. It was also a day of worship. Jesus himself went into the synagogues and temples on the sabbath to participate in the services.

Jesus carried forward the basic principle of the sabbath minus the innumerable irksome regulations formulated by Jewish scribes. For instance, under Jewish law one was permitted to enter fields to get food to sustain life, provided he only took what he could eat (Deut. 23:24). But to pluck grain on the sabbath was prohibited, being interpreted as work. Thus, when Jesus' disciples plucked grain on the sabbath, they were attacked by the Pharisees. Jesus justified their action by pointing out that the Son of Man is Lord of the sabbath, that human needs come before religious institutions, and that it is lawful to do good on the sabbath (Mark 2:23 to 3:6; Matt. 12:1–14; Luke 6:1–11).

Hence, Jesus laid down no commands, rules, or liturgies applying to the observance of the Lord's day. Rather, he simply gave the basic principle that it is lawful to do good on this day.

In Christianity the Jewish sabbath was transmuted into the "Lord's day," or the first day of the week. This was the day of Christ's resurrection and therefore called the "Lord's day" (Rev. 1:10). Accordingly, the early church held its meetings on the "first day of the week" (Acts 20:7), and collections were taken on this day (1 Cor. 16:1–2).

Duties to Man

Commandment five.—"Honor your father and your mother, that your days may be long in the land which the Lord your God gives you" (Ex. 20:12). This mandate marks the transition from duties to God to those applying to people. This one expresses the principle of right family relationships. "Honor" to parents means to take them seriously.[4] To take parents seriously is to respect them as God's means of carrying forward the race and their contribution in terms of a rich social heritage which they make available to their offspring.

Involved in this fifth commandment is also the responsibility of the offspring to care for their aged and indigent parents. Jesus cites a tradition of the Jews aimed at getting around this responsibility (Mark 7:8–13). He makes it clear that the practice of "Corban" (an offering dedicated to God) cannot release a son from the obligation to support his parents.

The Decalogue in Deuteronomy adds the promise of length of days to those who honor parents (5:16). Here, of course, the promise is to the nation. Fidelity to this law of honor to parents insures continued national existence. Where family life is strong there will be a stable society in which long life can be enjoyed. Family solidarity among the Jews has been one of the reasons for their racial survival under suffering through the centuries. Conversely the society which destroys the family destroys itself.

Commandment six.—"You shall not kill" (Ex. 20:13). "Do no murder" is a truer translation, for the Hebrew term translated "kill" means "murder." Accidental killing, justifiable homicide, killing in war, and capital punishment, therefore, were not considered to be murder among the Hebrews (Num. 35:23; Ex. 21:12 f.; 22:2). While this law was primarily for the protection of life within the Jewish community, it embodies the universal principle of the sacredness of human personality. The truly sacred aspect of man is not so much his life as his personality and relationship to God. Murder annihilates this relationship by destroying the image of God in man (Gen. 9:6). It is on this theological basis only that our human objection to murder can be logically defended.[5]

Commandment seven.—"You shall not commit adultery" (Ex. 20:14). This law expresses the principle of the sacredness of the marriage relationship. Originally this injunction applied less to husband than to the wife.[6] The law took account not so much of the sin of impurity as a violation of property rights—a man's ownership of his wife. Later, however, the law was interpreted to be equally applicable to both man and woman, as we find in Leviticus 20:10 where adultery was to be punished with death in the case of both. The law required, therefore, purity of sex life before and after marriage on the part of both male and female. Jesus went to the root of this injunction and demanded purity of heart as well as action, equating the lustful look with the act of adultery (Matt. 5:28).

Commandment eight.—"You shall not steal" (Ex. 20:15). Protection of the right to personal property is the ethical principle embraced in this precept. It is a fundamental basis upon which the right to private property rests. To "steal" implies not only direct theft, but also stealing in the guise of sharp business practices, the use of office for private gain, or the exploitation of the weak and ignorant. Wealthy and powerful individuals have often been able to steal from the public without penalty. This law applies equally to everyone, regardless of method of stealing.

Wages must be duly paid (Lev. 19:13; Deut. 25:14; cf. James 5:4), and honest measure must be given (Deut. 25:13). Care of the poor is the responsibility of all who have this world's goods to share (Deut. 15:7–11). God thus must be glorified in the getting as well as the giving of wealth.

Commandment nine.—"You shall not bear false witness against your neighbor . . ." (Ex. 20:16). Obligation to bear a true testimony regarding one's neighbor is the principle of this law. Primarily, it forbids false witnessing against one's fellowman in a court of law. The plaintiff, defendant, and witness are bound to tell the truth and nothing but the truth in any trial. Its broader implications prohibit the sin of slander, tale-bearing, gossip, flattery, "character assassination." To destroy a man's character by a whispering campaign profits nothing. As Shakespeare put it:

> Who steals my purse steals trash;
> . . . .
> But he that filches from me my good name
> Robs me of that which not enriches him
> And makes me poor indeed.[7]

Duty to Self

Commandment ten.—"You shall not covet . . ." (Ex. 20:17). This final injunction of the Decalogue has to do with man's duty to himself. It forbids the inordinate desire for the wrong things (neighbor's wife, cattle, servants, and so on). To covet, then, means to set the heart upon, to pant after, an intensely personal desire striking at the attitudes rather than the actions of man. It is an inward motive which gives birth to the overt sins of murder, adultery, lying, and stealing as described in the previous commandments. Thus, the seat of covetousness is the human heart (Rom. 1:24). It is a subtle sin because desire under pressure may quickly "curdle into covetousness." [8] Paul himself declares that he would not have known covetousness to be a sin had it not been for this law forbidding it (Rom. 7:7). One may covet the best spiritual gifts, providing it be done in the spirit of love (1 Cor. 12:31 ff.).

The Ten Commandments reflect the highest ethical standards of the early period of the Hebrews. Grounded in the covenant relation to the living God, these laws are eternal and not merely human ideals. They are comprehensive in that they contain the fundamental duties of man to God, neighbor, and himself. Absolute loyalty to the sovereign God, worship in keeping with his spiritual nature, reverence for his name, the hallowing of his day, sum up man's religious duties. Respect for parents, personality, marriage, property, and truth are the distinctively ethical obligations of the Commandments. Commandment ten is a duty which a man has to himself because it is related primarily to the heart. He must avoid harboring inordinate desires for the possessions of his neighbors. Without these universal and basic principles, no individual or society can rise to the moral level which God requires of humanity.

References

1. A. R. Osborn, *Christian Ethics* (Oxford: University Press, 1940), p. 42.

2. See the "Ritual" (Ex. 34:10–28) and "Deuteronomic" (Deut. 5:6–21) Decalogues.

3. H. H. Rowley, *Moses and the Decalogue* (Manchester: University Press, 1951), p. 95.

4. E. M. Poteat, *Mandate to Humanity* (New York: Abingdon Press, 1953), p. 140.

5. See Elton Trueblood, *Foundations for Reconstruction* (New York: Harper & Bros., 1946), p. 64.

6. Rowley, *op. cit.,* p. 111.

7. *Othello,* Act III, Sc. 3, line 131.

8. Poteat, *op. cit.,* p. 211.

Recommended Reading

CHARLES, ROBERT H., *The Decalogue.* Edinburgh: T. & T. Clark Co., 1923.

DAVIDMAN, JOY, *Smoke on the Mountain: An Interpretation of the Ten Commandments.* Philadelphia: Westminster Press, 1954.

POTEAT, E. M., *Mandate to Humanity.* New York: Abingdon Press, 1953.

ROWLEY, H. H., *Moses and the Decalogue.* Manchester: Manchester University Press, 1951.

TRUEBLOOD, ELTON, *Foundations for Reconstruction.* New York: Harper & Bros., 1946.

IV

Ethics of the Prophets

Hebrew morality reaches its high-water mark in the teachings of the prophets from about 800 to 400 B.C. Among these men are Isaiah, Amos, Hosea, Micah, and Jeremiah who reflect strong social passion and concern. Theirs is not an academic or speculative morality but one grounded in the righteous and living God. Not only are they interpreters of the faith but also moral analysts interested in economic, political, and social issues.[1]

The Prophet's Milieu

An understanding of the Hebrew prophet's socio-historical situation is essential to an appreciation of his mission and message. His days were characterized by dynamic change and social upheaval. The Israelites had moved from a semi-nomadic tribal life to a more settled agrarian and urban culture. Hence, economic, political, and social tensions were inevitable. These changes profoundly affected the religion and morals of the people. Politically, Israel had shifted from a theocracy to a monarchy, eventually becoming involved in international affairs. In the political upheavals which marked the period, she became, in succession, a vassal to Assyria, Babylon, and Persia. Jerusalem was destroyed in 587 B.C. and the leading citizens deported to Babylon. After the return from Exile in 537 B.C., the Jews began to rebuild their Holy City.

Religiously, the people kept up a form of faith which had little to do with righteousness in actual practice. The faith which had been "ethicised at Sinai had become materialised in Canaan, and mechanical relations had been substituted for relations that

26

were originally personal." [2] And the religion of Jehovah had become "homogenized" with the heathen religion of the Canaanites. Wealth had concentrated rapidly into the hands of the few. Greedy landowners oppressed and impoverished the masses. Courts were corrupt and the judges welcomed bribes; drunkenness was widespread among both men and women. Both capital cities, Samaria and Jerusalem, were shockingly corrupt. Rulers lived in luxury and were insensitive to the plight of the people (Amos 6:1–6). Against this background the Hebrew prophets arose to speak with judgment and hope.

The Prophet and His Role

The term "prophet" (*nabi'*) as used in the Old Testament applies to one who speaks on behalf of God to his people. The prophet's words are God's, not his own. Hence, his message is usually prefaced with "Thus saith the Lord." The prophet is conscious of a divine call. Amos, the herdsman, yields reluctantly to God's call to "go, prophesy to my people" (Amos 7:15). He declares, "The Lord has spoken; who can but prophesy?" (Amos 3:8). Isaiah, the aristocrat, voluntarily accepts God's call for a spokesman. While worshiping in the temple, Isaiah hears the voice of God speaking: "whom shall I send, and who will go for us?" (Isa. 6:8). He replies: "Here I am! Send me." God answers: "Go, and say to this people . . ." (Isa. 6:9). Jeremiah learns that he was appointed a prophet to the nations even before he was born (Jer. 1:5). Complaining that he is young and does not know how to speak, God touches Jeremiah's mouth and says: "Behold, I have put my words in your mouth" (Jer. 1:9).

With the possible exception of Ezekiel, the prophets of the period under discussion are not "ordained ministers." Citizens, they are, called of God to speak his message to the people. Thus Amos announces: "I am no prophet, nor a prophet's son; but I am a herdsman, and a dresser of sycamore trees, and the Lord took me from following the flock" (Amos 7:14–15). In other words, he refuses to be classified as a professional prophet.

Unfortunately, the conception of the prophet as a sort of a crystal-gazer, wholly devoted to predicting the future, is still

among us. But the eighth-century prophets are not so much pre-
dictors of the future as proclaimers to the present. Primarily
spokesmen to their own generation, the prophets tackle the current issues of the day. More than this, they are interpreters of the
past, citing God's acts in dealing with the people as a way of revealing divine meaning in history. For example, Jeremiah attributes Jerusalem's fall to Israel's idolatry (Jer. 44:2–6). Moreover, God's wrath on the wickedness of Shiloh is to be the fate of
Israel (Jer. 7:12–15). To some extent, the prophets are pre-
dictors of the future, near and far distant. Amos, for example,
predicts the imminent Assyrian invasion of western Asia and the
conquest and downfall of Israel (Amos 7:7 ff.). Micah, in 700
B.C., foresees the birth of Christ in Bethlehem (Mic. 5:2; cf.
Matt. 2:6). Isaiah's vision of a warless world is yet to be fulfilled
(Isa. 2:1 ff.).

Both true and false prophets operated in Israel. Jeremiah has
tests for detecting the false prophet. Such a prophet is not called
of God, yet he pretends to speak for him (Jer. 23:31); he cries,
"peace" when there is no peace (Jer. 6:14); his conception of
God is narrow and nationalistic. He teaches that God is bound to
protect Israel in all situations. Moreover, the false prophet does
not speak out against sin and evil, but rather accentuates complacency and condones corruption among the leaders of Israel. Jeremiah concludes that the false prophet is nothing but a "windbag"
(Jer. 5:13, Moffatt).

Theological Presuppositions and Ethical Principles

Though not theologians in the strictest sense of the word, the
Hebrew prophets' oracles are loaded with the stuff of theology.
In the prophetic apprehension, God is creator of all existence
(Jer. 27:5). He is omniscient, transcendent as well as imma-
nent: "Am I a God at hand, says the Lord, and not a God afar
off? Can a man hide himself in secret places so that I cannot see
him? . . . Do I not fill heaven and earth?" (Jer. 23:23–24). In
addition, he is sovereign of the nations and acts justly and re-
demptively in human history (Amos 9:7; Isa. 43:1).

The prophets carry forward the theological presuppositions

of the covenant and the election. A new emphasis is given to sin as rebellion against God and stemming from a corrupt heart. The day of the Lord is seen as one of darkness and not light (Amos 5:18–20). Israel will be carried away into captivity, but restoration is promised. A remnant will be saved. A day is coming when God will make a new covenant with his people, a covenant written upon the heart. This covenant will make possible an intimate personal fellowship between God and his children (Jer. 31:31–34). And it will pave the way for the ideal kingdom to be achieved through God's Messiah (Isa. 9:6–7).

Ethically, the prophets emphasized the principles of justice, righteousness, mercy, and love. Central in Amos is the demand for justice; Hosea stresses love; Isaiah holiness, Jeremiah and Ezekiel the responsibility of the individual before God. Micah summarizes the essence of religion in ethical terms: "He has showed you, O man, what is good; and what does the Lord require of you but to do justice, and to love kindness, and to walk humbly with your God?" (Mic. 6:8). Thus to be in step with God is to be related to him in ethical terms. Ritual is no substitute for justice (Amos 5:21–24), for positive defense of the weak (Isa. 1:10–17), and for personal purity (Hos. 4:12).

Problems of the Prophet

Society's spiritual and moral foundations in the days of the prophets were eaten away by the acids of injustice and unfaithfulness to God. The times were "out of joint." Therefore, the prophets were passionately concerned about the reconstruction of the social order in harmony with the will of God. For them it was "a religious imperative that society should be ordered as to make possible and to support a way of life which is *good* in the eyes of Yahweh." [3] God himself was understood to be in the struggle for social justice and an order of relationships among men in which his righteousness could find fulfilment.

Thus the prophets were private men interested in public morality, not mere "pie in the sky." They brought religious principles to bear upon political and social issues. For example, a genuine concern was expressed for the welfare of the family.

The family was viewed as the basic unit of society and they sought to preserve its integrity. Marriage was conceived of in monogamic terms. Polygamy, at least by inference, was frowned upon. There is no record that any prophet from Amos to Malachi had more than one wife. Divorce was denounced as a thing which God hates (Mal. 2:14–16). Adultery and prostitution in both men and women were sternly condemned (Jer. 7:9–10; Mal. 3:5). So sacred was the marriage relationship that it was used as a symbol of the relation of Yahweh to his people (Hos. 2:19–20; Jer. 2:1–7).

Again, the prophets inveighed against economic injustice. In unforgettable terms they denounced dishonest business practices. God spoke through Amos' words to greedy and deceitful merchants:

Hear this, you who trample upon the needy, and bring the poor of the land to an end, saying, "When will the new moon be over, that we may sell grain? And the sabbath, that we may offer wheat for sale, that we may make the ephah small and the shekel great, and deal deceitfully with false balances, that we may buy the poor for silver and the needy for a pair of sandals, and sell the refuse of the wheat?" (Amos 8:4–6).

These businessmen were so greedy for gain that they begrudged having to wait for the sabbath to pass!

Exploitation of the laboring man was vehemently condemned. The hireling must not be oppressed in his wages (Mal. 3:5). Aristocratic land-grabbers were denounced for joining "house to house" until the rural area was turned into a series of great estates reducing the farmers to the status of slaves (Isa. 5:8). Woes were pronounced upon those "who devise wickedness and work evil upon their beds! When the morning dawns, they perform it, because it is in the power of their hand" (Mic. 2:1). God threatened to pour out his wrath "like water" upon the princes of Judah who removed the landmarks and oppressed the weak (Hos. 5:10–11).

From the beginning of the Hebrew prophetic movement, politics was one of the major problems of the prophets. They set and upset kings and governments. Samuel anointed Saul the first king over Israel (1 Sam. 11:1–11). Nathan, the prophet, started a movement in favor of Solomon for the kingship of Israel (1 Kings 1). Elijah and Elisha sought to overthrow the house of Ahab (1 Kings 19:16; 2 Kings 9:1 ff.). Isaiah, the statesman-prophet, gave guidance to the state in time of crisis. His political philosophy was summed up in his words to King Ahaz during the Syro-Ephramatic invasion of Israel in 735 B.C. He advised: "Take heed, be quiet, do not fear, and do not let your heart be faint because of these two smoldering stumps of firebrands, at the fierce anger of Rezin and Syria and the son of Remaliah" (Isa. 7:4).

Crooked political officials came in for a tongue lashing by the prophets. Judges were accused of turning "justice to wormwood," and casting down the righteous of the earth (Amos 5:7). According to Isaiah, the rulers were "companions of thieves" (Isa. 1:23). For they perverted equity and built Zion with blood and Jerusalem with wrong (Mic. 3:9). So voracious were these political leaders that Micah likened them to cannibals "who eat the flesh of my people, and flay their skin from off them, and break their bones in pieces, and chop them up like meat in a kettle, like flesh in a caldron" (Mic. 3:1–3).

Complacency, luxury, and debauchery of the rulers in the capital cities of Samaria and Jerusalem were not overlooked by the prophets. The rulers were "at ease in Zion," and secure in the Mountain of Samaria. Meat from the choice lambs and calves was theirs. Instead of drinking wine from "cocktail glasses," they gulped it down by the bowlful. "Idle songs were sung" (bawled) to the sound of music. David used music for the worship of God, but these drunkards used musical instruments to accompany their bawling while on drinking sprees. They anointed themselves with the finest ointments. So blinded by luxury and corruption, these leaders of Israel were neither grieved at the affliction of the people nor aware of the approaching day of judgment (Amos 6:1–14).

Wicked women also came under the condemnation of the prophets. The rich women of Samaria were denounced by Amos with unsurpassed sarcasm. They reminded him of the sleek, fat cows of Bashan (Amos 4:1–3; cf. Deut. 32:14). Indirectly through their husbands, whom they compelled to bring home more money for strong drink, these women oppressed the poor and crushed the needy. But they would be led away by the enemy through open breaches in the wall of the city as unruly cattle.

Even as Amos attacked the women of Samaria for their oppression of the poor, Isaiah assailed the wickedness of the women of Jerusalem. Haughty and disdainful, these women lived in lazy luxury. The prophet gave a long list of the forms of dress and adornment worn by these women, many of which were worn by the heathen goddess Ishtar. A rich woman's whole wardrobe is described: anklets, headbands, crescents, pendants, bracelets, scarfs, headresses, armlets, sashes, perfume boxes, amulets, signet rings, nose rings, festal robes, mantles, cloaks, handbags, garments of gauze, linen garments, turbans, and veils (Isa. 3:18–20). But the prophet declared that the Lord will take away the finery of these evil women: "Instead of perfume there will be rottenness; and instead of a girdle, a rope; and instead of well-set hair, baldness; and instead of a rich robe, a girding of sackcloth; instead of beauty, shame" (Isa. 3:24–25).

Religious leaders were not spared by the prophets. Priests were denounced because they taught for hire. Prophets were condemned for divining for money. Priest and prophet yet had the gall to say, "Is not the Lord in the midst of us? No evil shall come upon us" (Mic. 3:11).

Finally, there was the problem of the individual. Prior to the Exilic prophets, the concept of Israel as a corporate personality prevailed among the Hebrews. The individual's primary identity was derived from the fact that he was a part of a psychic whole or unity so that the family, the clan, and the nation was seen as a single personality. The *nephesh* (soul) of the whole was in the individual. A corollary to this concept was the view that man's sins were to be punished or his good acts rewarded through his children. Hence, the whole family was sometimes charged with the sin of an individual member. One of the best examples of this idea in practice is found in Joshua 7:22–26.

With Jeremiah and Ezekiel came the rise of the doctrine of the individual, and, consequently, the responsibility of the individual for his own sins. Factors which made for the development of this doctrine were economic, political, and social.[4] Land ownership and commerce furnished the individual with opportunity for individual effort in enterprise. In the organization of a standing army, clans were disregarded (1 Sam. 8:12). Centralized worship and government in Jerusalem and consequent intercourse of people all over Israel contributed to the breakdown of narrow clanishness and provincialism. The Exile experience gave impetus to the disintegration of family and tribal ties. Lack of a central place of worship in Babylon threw the Jews back upon their own individual resources in the worship of God. Each man was forced to look at his own personal accountability to God.

Ezekiel, pastor to the Exiles, brought individualism into clearest focus, laying down the principles that every soul must stand before God on his own. It is summed up as follows: "Behold, all souls are mine; the soul of the father as well as the soul of the son is mine: the soul that sins shall die" (Ezek. 18:4; cf. Jer. 31:30). Hence, the proverb, "The fathers have eaten sour grapes, and the children's teeth are set on edge," repeated by the Jews to blame their sins on their fathers could no longer be used. For the righteousness of a father cannot save a sinful son, nor will the sins of a wicked father be visited upon the son (Ezek. 18:20 ff.). From henceforth the new Israel is to be a group of individuals in right relation to God to promote the good community.

The Contribution of the Prophets

Professor Arnold Toynbee has set up a scale for judging whose influence is most likely to last through the ages. He concludes that the works of the artists and men of letters outlive the deeds of businessmen, soldiers, and statesmen. The poets and the philosophers outrange the historian; while the prophets and saints overtop and outlast them all. Specifically, he notes that the prophets of Israel are among the greatest benefactors to our generation.[5] Many of their contributions are permanent and relevant for every age. They rooted human behavior in the righteousness of God. Religion was saved from legalism and ceremonialism. Conscience was made the seat of true religion. Faith became a matter of inward fellowship with God rather than obedience to external rules and codes. Each person was made responsible to God for his own sins. The particularistic view of God in early Hebrew thought was overcome. God was seen to demand moral and religious responsibility of all nations. And finally, the prophets declared that religion and morality are inseparable, redirecting Hebrew thought from ritual to an ethico-religious emphasis.

References

1. See John Skinner, *Prophecy and Religion: Studies in the Life of Jeremiah* (Cambridge: The University Press, 1922), Chapter 8, "The Prophet as a Moral Analyst."
2. John Patterson, *The Goodly Fellowship of the Prophets* (New York: Charles Scribner's Sons, 1950), p. 3.
3. R. B. Y. Scott, *The Relevance of the Prophets* (New York: Macmillan Co., 1944), p. 158.
4. Cf. J. M. Powis Smith, *The Prophet and His Problems* (New York: Charles Scribner's Sons, 1914), Chapter VII.
5. A. J. Toynbee, *Civilization on Trial* (New York: Oxford University Press, 1958), pp. 5 and 156.

Recommended Reading

CALKINS, RAYMOND, *The Modern Message of the Minor Prophets.* New York: Harper & Bros. 1947.

HYATT, J. P., *Prophetic Religion.* New York: Abingdon-Cokesbury Press, 1947.

PATTERSON, JOHN, *The Goodly Fellowship of the Prophets.* New York: Charles Scribner's Sons, 1950.

SCOTT, R. B. Y., *The Relevance of the Prophets.* New York: Macmillan Co., 1944.

SMITH, J. M. POWIS, *The Prophet and His Problems.* New York: Charles Scribner's Sons, 1914.

V

Ethics of the Sages

After the return from Exile, a large body of wisdom literature developed in Israel. Job, some of the Psalms, Proverbs, Ecclesiastes, and the Song of Songs comprise this body of writings. The wisdom literature is so called due to the fact that therein the Hebrew wise men present the nature and application of their findings on questions of religious and moral philosophy. H. Wheeler Robinson defines Israel's wisdom as *"the discipline whereby was taught the application of prophetic truth to the individual in the light of experience."* [1] The sages took the teachings of the prophets, individualizing and expressing them in more philosophical terms. Hence, their writings have been called "the philosophy of the Old Testament." It is not, however, a speculative philosophy, for it seeks in the light of God's will, to understand the true meaning of existence.

Hebrew wisdom, therefore, has a profound theological basis. God is creator and controller of all animate and inanimate nature (Prov. 3:19 f.; Job 9:4–10; Eccl. 3:11). He is all-wise, universal, incomprehensible, just, merciful, protector of the poor, a steadfast guide to the righteous (Prov. 15:3; Eccl. 7:13 f.; Prov. 16:11; 3:6). Of man God demands trust, reverence, patience, righteousness, the consecration of wealth and service (Prov. 3:5 f.; 9:10; 3:11–12).

As has been indicated, the wisdom of Israel is practical rather than speculative. In this sapient teaching, practical ethics comprehends all classes, conditions, and social relations of people. Human existence, therefore, in all of its relationships is viewed from the perspective of theistic and moral principles.

35

The Ethics of Job

Contrary to popular belief, the central theme of the book of Job is not suffering, but the true motive of morality. This motive is defined as "disinterested loyalty to God, which finds its own reward in serving still." [2] In genuine morality man serves God from a heart of love, not for the hope of reward. Job is a dramatic illustration of this truth. "Doth Job serve God for nought?" asks Satan. To settle this question, God permits Satan to test Job to ascertain whether this man's goodness is due to the fact that God has prospered him. As a result, Job is stripped of his wealth, family, health, and subjected to great suffering.

Four theories are given for Job's pain and misery: first, a test of character (1:11 f.; 2:4 f.); second, a punishment for sin as suggested by Job's three friends, which is the traditional view (4:7-9; 5:17 f.; 9:22; 10:1-15; 12:5 f.); third, a warning to the straying man as seen in the speech of Elihu (33:14-30); and fourth, as a means of self-understanding and a more vital personal relationship to God (Job 42:5-6). Job takes the last position: "I had heard of thee by the hearing of the ear, but now my eye sees thee; therefore I despise myself, and repent in dust and ashes."

Job emerges from his suffering maintaining his integrity. His is not a *quid pro quo* religion. It is, as John F. Genung says, "A heart-loyalty, a hunger after God's presence, which survives loss and chastisement." [3] In Job's experience, all utilitarian motives in religion are set aside, and service to God free from self-interest becomes the heart of faith.

Chapter 31 contains an excellent statement of Job's ethics. It gives insight into the character of the man himself. Truly evangelical in its standards, there is much in this chapter which corresponds with the ethics of the New Testament. Job is free from immorality, including the lustful look (1-4), falsehood, deceit, and adultery which is conceived as a heinous crime (5-12). His slaves are never treated unjustly (13-15). The poor, the widow, and fatherless are objects of his benevolence (16-23). He does not rejoice in his great wealth or go after idols (24-28). He is not happy at the destruction of his enemy and his door is open to the stranger (29–34). Public indictment would not embarrass Job, for he would gladly give an account of his daily conduct (35–36). He concludes by saying:

> If my land has cried out against me,
>   and its furrows have wept together;
> if I have eaten its yield without payment,
>   and caused the death of its owners;
> let thorns grow instead of wheat,
>   and foul weeds instead of barley (38–40).

Job is saying, in effect, that even if his land had a voice it could not charge him with injustice.

The Ethics of the Psalms

Among the wisdom Psalms are 1, 10, 15, 37, 49, 73, 90, 111, 112, and 119. A prevalent problem in some of these psalms is that of the prosperity of wicked men. Puzzled about God's inactivity in dealing with such men, the psalmist asks: "Why dost thou stand afar off, O Lord? Why dost thou hide thyself in times of trouble?" (10:1). In the sanctuary of the Lord, the psalmist finds the answer: "Then I perceived their end . . . thou dost make them fall to ruin" (Psalm 73:17–18). The truly prosperous, therefore, are those who make God their guide (73:24–28).

Philosophical attitudes are reflected in Psalms 14, 19, and 90. Here the psalmist contemplates the good God and the godless world—God's revelation to man, and his eternity in contrast to man's ephemeral existence. Psalms 111 and 112 express praise for the great work of God along with a portrait of the good man. The good man endures, is generous, just, steady at heart, and held in honor. To him a "light rises in the darkness."

The Ethics of Proverbs

Proverbs is almost wholly a book of practical morality. Its theme is "the worth of wisdom." Wisdom is personified in a beautiful woman, Lady Wisdom, who has around her the virtues of the wise: humility, kindness, justice, love of enemies, mercy, sobriety, chastity, discreet speech. Folly is personified by another woman, Lady Folly, who is surrounded by the vices of the foolish man: anger, pride, envy, jealousy, lying, idleness, drunkenness, sexual immorality, crime, injustice. Each personified figure prepares a banquet and offers invitation to "the simple one."

The whole range of human relations is seen in the light of wisdom and practical ethics. But morality is more than an intellectual matter because it has a religious basis. The "fear of the Lord" is the very beginning of wisdom (Prov. 1:7). True knowledge, therefore, is the practical understanding and obedience of God's will as the law of life.

The family.—Family life is given a prominent emphasis in Proverbs. Among ancient civilizations no more exalted place is given the woman than in this book. A portrait of a worthy woman is presented in chapter 31:10–31. She is seen to be in her finest role as one who "buildeth her house." Her home is her throne and glory. The heart of her husband trusts in her. She is industrious, has business ability, and is generous to the poor. Strength and dignity are her clothing. She opens her mouth with wisdom, and the law of kindness is on her tongue. She does not eat the bread of idleness; her children rise up and call her blessed. Her husband can say, "Many women have done excellently, but you surpass them all" (31:29).

The contentious woman is a source of family tensions. A wife's quarreling is like "a continual dripping of rain" (19:13). The sage concludes: "It is better to live in a corner of the housetop than in a house shared with a contentious woman" (25:24).

The husband is expected to be faithful. Infidelity is both sinful and foolish, for the man who is unfaithful has "no sense" and "destroys himself" (6:32). There is no specific reference to polygamy in Proverbs and monogamous marriage appears to be taken for granted (cf. 5:18).

The family is regarded as a school and its life as a discipline (Prov. 22:6). The father is expected to wisely discipline his children. With regard to the method, moral suasion is better than lashes. Yet the rod may be necessary at times (13:24; 19:18). A sound threshing will not kill the child and may save his life from Sheol (23:13). It appears that the sages had no fear of children suffering from inhibitions and complexes caused by their natural impulses.

Children are expected to respect and obey their parents (1:8–9; 3:1 f.; 15:20; 20:20). Among the four classes of detestable persons are children who curse their parents (30:11). Other sins against parents specially condemned are mocking, despising, using violence, scorning instruction, and robbery (19:26; 30:17; 13:1; 28:24). The wise son makes his father happy, but the foolish one is a sorrow to his mother (10:1; 15:20).

The duty of the father to be a good provider is taken for granted. The lazy man is intolerable. He turns over in bed without getting up to work "as a door turns on its hinges," and it is a burden to him to lift his hand from his dish to his mouth (26:14–15). He is advised to take a lesson from the ant (6:6–8).

Business life.—Wisdom has its implications for business practices and the uses of wealth. Oppression of the poor to increase one's own wealth results in want of the oppressor (22:16). Sharp business dealings are condemned: " 'It is bad, it is bad,' says the buyer; but when he goes away, then he boasts" (20:14). "A false balance is an abomination to the Lord, but a just weight is his delight" (11:1). Wisdom is opposed to those who remove the ancient landmark and devour the poor off the earth (22:28; 30:14). The sage concludes: "Better is a little with righteousness than great revenues with injustice" (16:8).

Great wealth exposes one to the danger of being full and denying the Lord. Extreme poverty tempts one to dishonesty (30:8–9). Hence the wise man desires neither poverty nor wealth, but only to be fed with the food needful for him. He who has money should use it to help the poor, for "He who is kind to the poor lends to the Lord, and he will repay him for his deed" (19:17).

The state.—Little is said in Proverbs about the state and political problems. The wicked ruler is portrayed as "a roaring lion" over the poor people (28:15). The good king depends upon God, is righteous, wise, trustful, and merciful (16:10; 20:26, 28; 31:1–9). Corrupt politicians accept "a bribe from the bosom to pervert the ways of justice" (17:23). Goodness is essential to national prosperity: "Righteousness exalts a nation, but sin is a reproach to any people" (14:34). Conservative in politics, the sage discourages violence and revolution: "My son, fear thou the Lord and the king: and meddle not with them that are given to change" (24:21, KJV).

The Ethics of Ecclesiastes

Ecclesiastes, or the Preacher, is "a Hebrew philosopher" searching for the *summum bonum* of life. He desires to know what is "good for the sons of men to do . . ." (2:3).

Four quests for the real profit of life are made. The first is by the philosophical approach (1:12–18); second is through the pursuit of pleasure (2:1–11); third is through work and wealth (2:18 to 6:12); and fourth is by the path of fame (7:1 to 11:8).

After each quest the searcher concludes that "all is vanity and a striving after the wind." Thus the writer refutes secularism on its own ground.

Then is life worth living? After a serious study of this question, the author gives an affirmative reply. He declares that the end of the whole matter is to "fear God, and keep his commandments; for this is the whole duty of man" (12:13).

The Ethics of The Song of Songs

The Song of Songs contains an ethical gem in its theme—the faithfulness of true love. Regardless of which theory one takes as to the form of the poem—the drama, the allegory, or the collection of wedding songs—its main purpose is to emphasize the purity and strength of true love. It excludes polygamy and exalts true love, marital loyalty, and an exclusive devotion between lovers. These facts alone are sufficient to justify a place for these songs in the canon of the Scriptures. As against the romantic notion of love so prevalent in our present society, the Song of Songs offers the concept of love which is stronger than death. In the following verses is found one of the most beautiful descriptions of love ever written.

Set me as a seal upon your heart, as a seal upon your arm; for love is strong as death, jealousy as cruel as the grave. Its flashes are flashes of fire, a most vehement flame. Many waters cannot quench love, neither can floods drown it. If a man offered for love all the wealth of his house, it would be utterly scorned (8:6–7). ·

We have attempted to point up the ethical principles of the Old Testament. A summary of these moral truths will help us to keep in focus norms of behavior which God requires of his people. The integrating ethical concept of the Old Covenant is the will of God rather than the reason of man. The content of God's will is love, loyalty, righteousness, and justice as expressed in the Law, the Prophets, and the Wisdom Writings. These basic principles are sometimes obscured by the covering of legalism which developed in later Judaism. One of the moral contributions of Jesus was to dig beneath the vast debris of traditions, laws, and codes which had accrued to the will of God and to bring to light its true meaning and relevance.

References

1. H. W. Robinson, *Inspiration and Revelation in the Old Testament* (Oxford: Clarendon Press, 1946), p. 241.
2. *Ibid.*, p. 246.
3. J. F. Genung, *The Epic of the Inner Life* (New York: Houghton Mifflin Co., 1893), p. 20.

Recommended Reading

DAVIDSON, W. T., *The Wisdom Literature of the Old Testament*. London: Charles Kelly, 1894.
RANKIN, O. C., *Israel's Wisdom Literature; Its Bearing on Theology and the History of Religion,* Edinburgh: T. & T. Clark, 1936.
RANSTON, HARRY, *The Old Testament Wisdom Books and Their Teaching.* London: Epworth Press, 1930.

VI

Essential Character of Christ's Ethics

Jesus Christ is the full-orbed revelation of God's will and way (Heb. 1:1–2). In him the moral teachings of the Law, the prophets, and the sages find their fulfilment. In him the Law is perfectly fulfilled (Matt. 5:17–20). To him "all the prophets bear witness" (Acts 10:43). The justice of Amos, the love of Hosea, the holiness of Isaiah, and the wisdom of the sages are gathered up in Christ and their divine fulness is revealed. Christ is the wisdom of God, being made our wisdom, righteousness, sanctification, and redemption (1 Cor. 1:24–30).

This chapter deals with the nature of Jesus' ethics. Jesus as a teacher of morality, the chief characteristics of his moral teaching, and its relation to the kingdom of God are described.

The Master Teacher of Morality

The term "teacher" (*didaskalos*) was frequently applied to Jesus (Mark 4:38; Mark 12:32; John 3:2). More references appear in the Gospels to his teaching than to his preaching. As a teacher, Jesus' message was not only one of redemption but also one of righteousness. He was concerned not only with telling people how to be "saved" but also with teaching them how to live in society.

As a teacher of ethics, Jesus used sound educational methods.[1] In his "school" there was created a learning atmosphere. The disciples enjoyed the elements of fellowship and freedom of

42

thought. Jesus employed the Socratic question and answer method by which students were drawn into dialogic encounters with himself and with one another. He taught with clarity, using language the people could understand. To make his teachings easier to grasp and to retain, Jesus made use of the parable, proverb, and poem. And, in keeping with the best educational methods of teaching, he stimulated his disciples to think for themselves, to form positive convictions, and to act accordingly.

The fact that Jesus taught great ethical principles rather than rules gave his ethic validity and permanency. His teaching was confined to eternal values devoid of the legalism and the unscientific views of the universe which were characteristic of his time. Therefore, there is a timelessness in Jesus' ethics which is free from purely local and temporal conditions.

There is also finality in the ethics of Jesus. His lofty ethical ideals have never been superseded. They transcend all time, space, and scientific progress. As Goethe said, "Let intellectual and spiritual culture progress, and the human mind expand, as much as it will; beyond the grandeur and the moral culture of Christianity, as it sparkles and shines in the Gospels, the human mind will not advance." [2] Indeed, Jesus' great ethical principles of the value of the individual, the brotherhood of man, and the "Golden Rule" are even taught in the name of science.[3] Jesus is truly the Master Teacher of the moral life.

"Out of His Treasure Things Old and New"

Some scholars challenge the claim of any uniqueness in the ethic of Jesus. Joseph Klausner, a Jewish thinker, declares that *"throughout the Gospels there is not one item of ethical teaching which cannot be paralleled either in the Old Testament, the Apocrypha, or in the Talmudic and Midrashic literature of the period near to the time of Jesus."* [4] Admittedly, Jesus did not begin his ethical teaching *de novo*. Many of his moral ideas can be found in Jewish writings. Certainly he borrowed from the Old Testament, especially from the Prophets and Writings, and the Psalms. But out of this great storehouse of moral treasure Jesus brought forth new emphases and distinctive truths.

For one thing, Jesus placed a new emphasis upon the inseparable relation between theology and ethics. He grounded morality in the God of righteousness and love. Morality, as Jesus taught it, is radically theocentric, as evidenced in the statement that we are to be perfect as our Father in heaven is perfect (Matt. 5:48). God himself, and not man, is the measure of all morality. Efforts, therefore, to divorce Jesus' ethics from his theology do violence to his message. As T. W. Manson says,

> The notion that we can wander at will through the teaching of Jesus as through a garden, plucking here and there an ethical flower to weave a chaplet for the adornment of our own philosophy of life, is an idea that is doomed to disappointment, for the nature of plucked flowers is to wither. The ethical maxims of Jesus, abstracted from the religion out of which they grow, become mere counsels of perfection which we may indeed respectfully admire, but which have no immediate reference to the affairs of our ordinary life.[5]

Thus, without the energy which comes from faith in God, the ethics of Jesus—like all speculative ethics—becomes a theoretical abstraction.

The ethics of Jesus is distinctive in that it is primarily for redeemed persons who have been regenerated by the power of the Holy Spirit (John 3:3). Thus Jesus linked morality with "a new religious experience."[6] This wedding of morality with the radical transformation of the individual is unique in religious thought. This new life is possible only through repentance, "the one and only door of salvation into the Kingdom."[7]

Jesus laid stress upon the inwardness of morality and the motives of men. To be angry at someone is to be guilty of murder, and to look lustfully upon a woman is to commit adultery in the heart (Matt. 5:21–30). W. F. Lofthouse asserts that Jesus' insistence "on turning from the act which a judge might deal with, to the motive, which lies outside the range of law" cannot be paralleled in any Jewish writing.[8]

The value of the individual was given a new emphasis in Jesus' teaching. Adolph Harnack claims that Jesus was "the first to bring the value of every human soul to light."[9] Jesus taught that men are of more value than animals and that the life of one person is worth more than the world (Matt. 12:12; Mark 8:36). He saw worth in a repulsive leper, healed him and returned him to society (Matt. 8:1–4). He forgave a wasted woman and put her accusers to shame (John 8:1 f.). While the disciples felt that little children were too insignificant to bring to Jesus' attention, he saw in them the possibilities of the kingdom of God (Mark 10:13–16). Physical deformity, moral guilt, and age did not obscure for Jesus the sacredness of personality. "For God's temple is holy, and that temple you are" (1 Cor. 3:16).

Jesus' morality was characterized by a positiveness which is lacking in other religions. He manifested a genuine contempt for mere negative goodness. The positive nature of his teaching is seen specifically in the "Golden Rule" (Matt. 7:12; Luke 6:31); in his concept of forgiveness which requires the offended to take the initiative in being reconciled to the offender (Matt. 5:23–25); and in his demand that the Christian's righteousness must exceed the negative righteousness of the scribes and Pharisees (Matt. 5:20).

Love was given a new dimension of meaning in Jesus' teaching. Popular Jewish thought tended to conceive love to neighbor as love to a fellow Hebrew. Jesus extended love to include everyone, even our enemies (Matt. 5:44). In the parable of the good Samaritan, Jesus plainly taught unqualified love to those of other races. But Jesus not only extended love to include everyone, he also gave love a new basis. We are to love one another as he loves us (John 13:34). Hence, the love that Jesus taught is unique, unqualified, and selfless. His new commandment of love, therefore, goes beyond mere love to neighbor as one loves himself, as stated in the "second commandment" (Matt. 22:39).

The ethics of Jesus contained a new and distinctive concept of service. When the disciples argued as to which one would be accounted greatest, Jesus said to them: "If any one would be first, he must be last of all and servant of all" (Mark 9:35). In John 13:4–5, Jesus gave them an example of service by taking a towel and washing their feet. And in Luke 22:25–27, he added a word of exhortation:

The kings of the Gentiles exercise lordship over them; and those in authority over them are called benefactors. But not so with you; rather let the greatest among you become as the youngest, and the leader as one who serves. For which is the greater, one who sits at table, or one who serves? Is it not the one who sits at table? But I am among you as one who serves.

Jesus' purpose in these passages was to teach self-abasing or lowly service as an act of love. He explained that true greatness in the kingdom of God comes, not from rank and power as measured by the secular world, but by service to others. No other religion possesses the concept of service with the unique meaning appearing here in the teaching of Jesus.

Finally, Jesus' life was in perfect harmony with his ethical ideals. "The whole of the active work of Jesus," as Hans Heinrich Wendt says, "was an exposition of his teaching with his own example." [10] There is no equivalent in any religion to this idea of the relation of Jesus to the ethics which he taught. Professor H. H. Henson points up this fact by saying that there is no other religion in which the historic founder is recognized "as a norm of personal morality . . . Jesus alone is able to offer himself as the sufficient illustration of his own doctrine." [11] Men have taught high ideals without perfectly demonstrating them in their personal lives. For instance, Plato, Socrates, Kant, and others spoke theoretically of a way of life, but the Christian ideal is manifested in the person of Jesus, the pattern of the perfect life. Hence, the ultimate norm of the Christian is not a rule, a creed, an ethical system, but a personality. Christ himself becomes the final criterion of all character and conduct.

"His Kingdom and His Righteousness"

The "magnificent obsession" of Jesus is the kingdom of God or heaven. It was central in his message and the objective of his mission. He referred to the church only twice (Matt. 16:18; 18:17) and to the kingdom more than 70 times. His gospel is defined as that of the kingdom (Matt. 4:23). Almost all of his parables deal with the kingdom.

Though Jesus never defined the kingdom, he did describe its

nature and demand. But it appears to be the kingly rule of God in Christ. Subjectively, the kingdom of God is the reign of Christ in the individual life. It exists objectively whether recognized or not, being in "our midst" and "at hand" (Luke 17:20-21; Mark 1:15). The objective aspect of the kingdom is sometimes identified as being communal in nature. T. W. Manson brings together both the personal and the communal aspects by saying:

Primarily the Kingdom is a personal relation between God as King and the individual as subject. Then it appears in the world as a society, something which might be called the People of God. This society consists of all those who are linked together by the fact of their common allegiance to one King.[12]

This communal theory presents a strong case, because the kingship of God cannot be exercised in a vacuum; it necessarily implies a kingdom, a community of subjects.[13] Of course, the kingdom cannot be wholly identified with the church as is done by the Roman Catholic theologians; but the church does appear to be the "out-cropping" of the kingdom. It is the realm in which God rules directly.

In contrast to the popular Jewish notion of a worldly, Davidic kingdom, Jesus conceived it to be spiritual, universal, and invisible (Matt. 8:11; Luke 17:20). The kingdom is both a present reality and a future hope (Mark 1:15; Luke 11:20; 17:21; Matt. 5:12; 12:28). It comes by growth and ultimately in the catastrophic manner by the power of God (Matt. 13:31 ff.; Mark 4:26–29; Luke 13:18–19). It is a gift of God and not achieved by the efforts of men (Luke 12:32). And it is clear that the kingdom is not to be identified with social progress or earthly institutions (John 18:36).

Though the kingdom is a gift from God, to receive it there are certain conditions to be fulfilled on man's part. To receive the kingdom one must repent and believe in the gospel (Mark 1:15), be born again (John 3:3–5), become as a little child (Matt. 18:3–4), and be willing to follow Jesus in the path of self-discipline, self-denial, and self-sacrifice (Mark 9:47–48; Matt. 19:29; Luke 9:61–62).

The supreme quest of the Christian is the kingdom of God and his righteousness (Matt. 6:33). In the Scriptures righteousness has a threefold meaning: soteriological (God's righteousness as deliverance or salvation); ethical (God's righteousness as a norm of conduct); eschatological (God's righteousness as the achievement of his purpose in history). Jesus conceives of righteousness in ethical terms as life in harmony with the will of God. His ethics is an exposition of the righteousness of the kingdom of God, the manner in which men behave when they submit to the kingship of Christ. Love of enemies, forgiveness, the golden rule, indeed the whole ethics of Jesus unfolds the meaning and brings out the implications of the kingly rule of God.

In contrast to Jewish ritualistic righteousness, Jesus teaches revolutionary righteousness. Jewish righteousness is external, legal, ceremonial conformity to the law. Jesus' righteousness is internal, spontaneous, never adherence to a fixed set of rules for behavior. In short, Jesus' righteousness is revolutionary moral practice, not ritual performance.

In contrast to our contemporary relativistic ethics, Jesus' norm is consistently the righteousness of God, not the customs of the community. God's children are to be holy as he is holy (Lev. 19:2; 1 Peter 1:16), perfect as he is perfect (Matt. 5:48), and merciful as he is merciful (Luke 6:36). The Christian's norm of righteousness, therefore, is not merely the folkways and mores of society, but the righteousness of the eternal God.

The "fruit of righteousness" is the gift of God which finds expression in many human forms such as love, humility, forgiveness, peace. The Sermon on the Mount defines the nature of God's righteousness and the manner in which it is expressed in character and conduct. Here the "fruit of righteousness" is systematically described. Hence, the next chapter is devoted to an interpretation of the moral meaning of the content of the Sermon.

References

1. See Luther Weigle, *Jesus and the Educational Method* (New York: Abingdon Press, 1939), Chapter I.

2. Cited by Adolph Harnack, *What Is Christianity?*, trans. T. B. Saunders (New York): Harper & Bros., 1957), p. 4.

3. Julian S. Huxley, *Evolutionary Ethics* (Oxford: Oxford University Press, 1943), p. 53. Also Robert A. Millikan, *Science and the New Civilization* (New York: Charles Scribner's Sons, 1930), section on "Three Great Elements in Human Progress."

4. Joseph Klausner, *Jesus of Nazareth* (New York: Macmillan Co., 1925), p. 384.

5. T. W. Manson, *The Teaching of Jesus; Studies of Its Form and Content* (Cambridge: University Press, 1935), p. 286.

6. Maurice Goguel, *The Life of Jesus,* trans. Olive Wyon (New York: Macmillan Co., 1933), p. 585.

7. Charles Guigenbert, *Jesus,* trans. S. H. Hooke (London: Kegan Paul, Trench, Trubner and Co., 1935), p. 403.

8. "Biblical Ethics," *A Companion to the Bible,* ed. T. W. Manson (Edinburgh: T. & T. Clark, 1936), p. 360.

9. Harnack, *op. cit.*

10. Hans Heinrich Wendt, *The Teaching of Jesus* (New York: Charles Scribner's Sons, 1899), I, 114.

11. H. H. Henson, *Christian Morality.* Oxford: Clarendon Press, 1936, p. 301.

12. Manson, *op. cit.,* p. 134.

13. *See* Vincent Taylor, *The Life and Ministry of Jesus* (New York: Abingdon Press, 1955), Chapter 15, for a summary of evidence in support of the communal aspect of the kingdom.

Recommended Reading

DODD, C. H., *Gospel and Law.* New York: Columbia University Press, 1951.

MANSON, T. W., *The Teaching of Jesus.* Cambridge: University Press, 1935.

MARSHALL, L. H., *The Challenge of New Testament Ethics.* New York: Macmillan Co., 1947, Chapter 1.

SCOTT, C. A. A., *New Testament Ethics.* Cambridge: University Press, 1936.

SCOTT, E. F., *The Ethical Teaching of Jesus.* New York: Charles Scribner's Sons, 1925.

VII
Content of Christ's Ethics

While the Sermon on the Mount in Matthew 5 to 7 is an incomplete statement of Jesus' ethic, it does present the essence of his moral teaching. Its central theme is the righteousness of the kingdom of God. Here is described the character and conduct of its citizens.

The Context of the Sermon

Setting the scene of the sermon requires a look at its background which begins with Matthew 4:23. Here Jesus is described as going about all Galilee teaching and preaching the gospel of the kingdom of God. This introductory section (Matt. 4:23 to 5:2) serves to indicate the theme of the sermon and, also, the fact that Jesus has reached the peak of his popularity.[1] When Jesus saw the multitudes, he retired to a hill, sat down (after the fashion of a Jewish teacher) and taught the disciples. Strictly speaking, therefore, the Sermon on the Mount is the "teaching on the hill" as a systematic statement of the main elements of the Christian ethic.

While Matthew 5:1 implies that Jesus removed with his disciples to the hill, Matthew 7:28 describes the astonishment of the crowd at his sayings. To whom, then, was the sermon addressed? Hans Windisch holds that the sermon was primarily addressed to the disciples, but that at the same time it was an "evangelistic" message directed to "the few and the all."[2] Bishop Charles Gore contends that the sermon was spoken "to the Church, not the world; but as the 'multitudes' appear also to have listened to it, we may say that it was spoken into the ear of the Church and overheard by the world." [3] We can safely conclude that the sermon was addressed primarily to the disciples but overheard by the crowds.

To get a perspective of the principal features of the sermon in Matthew 5 to 7 the following outline is presented:

1. Christian character (5:3–12)
2. Christian influence in the world (5:13–16)
3. Christian conduct (5:17 to 7:12)
   (1) The new criterion of conduct (5:17–20)
   (2) The new righteousness-ethic illustrated:
      a. In six antitheses contrasting the old righteousness and the new righteousness (5:21–48)
      b. In the true motive of worship (6:1–18)
      c. In allegiance, trust, and anxiety (6:19–34)
      d. In treatment of others (7:1–12)
4. Tests of character (7:13–27)
   (1) The two ways (7:13–14)
   (2) False teachers and false fruits (7:15–20)
   (3) Profession without practice (7:21–23)
   (4) The two houses (7:24–27)
5. Conclusion (7:28–29)

In the following pages the content of the sermon will be analyzed with particular attention to its great theme of righteousness in relation to Christian personality, the Law, and interpersonal relations.

The Content of the Sermon

We have indicated that the sermon contains material which describes the kingdom man and his manner of life. Its theme is the new righteousness of Christ in contrast to the old righteousness of the law. As the sermon unfolds, this higher righteousness is reflected in the Christian in terms of character, influence, worship, and relation to others, coming to a climax in the tests of his character.

Portrait of Christian Character (Matt. 5:3–12)

The Beatitudes present the essential elements of Christian character and portray the true righteous subject of the kingdom. The truly righteous are the poor in spirit, the mourners, the meek, those who hunger and thirst for righteousness, the merciful, the pure in heart, the peacemakers, the persecuted for righteousness' sake. To such persons is ascribed the term "blessed."

It is necessary to point out that the Greek word, *makarios,* translated "blessed," has nothing to do with happiness in the popular sense of pleasure and prosperity. Rather, it indicates an inner joy independent of outward circumstances. This blessedness is a present possession to be perfected in the future heavenly life.[4]

"Blessed are the poor in spirit . . ." (Matt. 5:3). Spiritual poverty is a basic element of Christian character. The poor in spirit are conscious of spiritual bankruptcy before God and feel their need of dependence upon him. In the parable of the Pharisee and the publican, the former felt no spiritual need. The publican, because he recognized his own spiritual impoverishment, went down from the temple justified rather than the Pharisee (Luke 18:10–14). Those who recognize their spiritual need, and realize their utter dependence upon the spiritual riches of God's grace, possess the kingdom of God.

"Blessed are those who mourn . . ." (Matt. 5:4). This beatitude refers not merely to that of funeral mourning, but to sorrow and suffering in general. It involves a sorrow for sin and a sharing in the sorrow of others. Christians are to bear one another's burdens as well as their own (Gal. 6:2–5). The God of all comfort "comforts us in all our affliction, so that we may be able to comfort those who are in any affliction, with the comfort with which we ourselves are comforted by God" (2 Cor. 1:3–4). That man is truly blessed who knows the comfort of God in the midst of sorrow and affliction.

"Blessed are the meek . . ." (Matt. 5:5). Meekness has become synonymous with weakness in our day. But the Greek word, *praus,* means far more than a groveling "goody-goody" person. The two basic ideas in the word *praus* are: (1) a readiness to obey God; and (2) a willingness to accept his discipline. Thus the meek or humble man is Christ-controlled in the totality of his life. Such persons can claim the promise that they shall inherit the earth. John W. Bowman suggests that, in this beatitude, "earth" is the equivalent of the kingdom of God and, therefore, the promise is essentially the same as found in the first beatitude.[5] More probably, "earth" refers to the "new earth," in which righteousness will dwell (2 Peter 3:13).

"Blessed are those who hunger and thirst for righteousness . . ." (Matt. 5:6). Hunger and thirst are strong terms expressing intense desire or craving. The righteous man has a passion for righteousness in the earth. Righteousness in this beatitude is more than a conventional standard of respectability. That man is truly righteous who is engaged in the struggle of right against wrong. He intensely desires the triumph of righteousness in every relationship in life. Those who have a strong appetite for righteousness and participate in the cause of righteousness shall be satisfied. Just as food and drink satisfy the physical, so righteousness gives satisfaction to the spiritual life.

"Blessed are the merciful . . ." (Matt. 5:7). Another element of Christian personality is mercifulness. Like righteousness, mercy is also active and social. It is possible to have a religion without active mercy, a creed without compassion, as seen in the parable of the good Samaritan (Luke 10:25 ff.). Priest and Levite, both religious leaders, left the robbed and wounded man by the side of the road without attempting to aid him. Theirs was a religion without active mercy. Since God himself is merciful, the children of his kingdom are to be merciful (Luke 6:36). Only those who show mercy will receive mercy. They receive mercy because their God is merciful.

"Blessed are the pure in heart . . ." (Matt. 5:8; cf. Psalm 24:3 f.). "Pure," from the Greek word *katharos,* means unadulterated and without alloy. Hence, the pure in heart have unmixed motives. Purity, then, is not an external quality, but an inward one. The Jews tended to think of purity as an external thing, secured by abstaining from certain foods, by avoiding all contact with dead bodies and Gentiles. Jesus made it clear that it is the sins of the heart which separate men from God (Mark 7:1–23). Only those who are pure in heart shall see God. The impure in heart are not aware of God's presence in the midst of life. But those with a pure heart recognize his presence even in sorrow and suffering and will one day see him face to face (Heb. 12:14; 1 John 3:2; Rev. 22:4).

"Blessed are the peacemakers . . ." (Matt. 5:9). Peacemaking is another trait of kingdom men. They not only possess peace in their hearts, but make peace among men. The blessing is on the peace*makers* not the "peace keepers." As peacemakers they have a twofold task: to work for right relationships between God and man, and between man and man. This is in harmony with God's great work of reconciling men to himself. Peacemakers thus are engaged in what God does and therefore are called "the sons of God." Those who divide people are doing the devil's work; those who reconcile men are doing God's work.[6]

"Blessed are those who are persecuted for righteousness' sake . . ." (Matt. 5:10). Joy in suffering is a characteristic of the Christian. Righteousness here does not refer to the righteousness of God, but to suffering in a just cause.[7] It is persecution for "righteousness' sake," not just any persecution, that is blessed. The New Testament seems to take for granted that those who live godly lives in Christ Jesus shall suffer persecution (2 Tim. 3:12). Certainly the Christian is not exempted from persecution when he stands for a righteous cause such as justice in racial, economic, and political relations. He will be slandered and abused if he challenges the *status quo* of society. But these persecuted are to rejoice, for their reward is great in heaven. They have the joy of sharing in the suffering of the prophets and of Jesus. Too, they have the promise of the presence of Christ and a sense of his guidance in their lives.

Jesus "unblushingly" appeals to reward as a motive.[8] But he never thinks in terms of "wage-theory righteousness." His is no *quid pro quo* morality. He does not share the old Hebrew concept of goodness as a good investment (Prov. 19:17; Matt. 6:4–18; Mark 10:29; Luke 6:35). The rewards to which Jesus appeals are spiritual and attract only those who aim at "a selfless ideal." [9] There is no question of "merit" in Jesus' teaching about reward. Those who practice piety for the hope of secular reward and esteem of men will get no other reward (Matt. 6:1 ff.). Jesus thus counsels men to do good to others with no hope of reward

(Luke 6:35), and reminds us that virtue at its highest is unconscious of itself (Matt. 25:31 ff.).

Citizens of the kingdom of God are the poor in spirit, the mourners, the humble, the merciful, the truly righteous, the peacemakers, and the persecuted. These persons are blessed now "for" theirs is the kingdom of heaven; they are comforted; they inherit the earth; they are satisfied; they obtain mercy; they see God; they are called the sons of God; their reward is great in heaven. The hope of the world lies in this type of personality.

Christian Influence in the World (Matt. 5:13–16)

The influence of kingdom men is described under the symbols of salt and light. Thus they are to be the preserving and enlightening forces of the world. Salt has a threefold function: penetration, purification, and preservation. Likewise, the "salty influence" of the Christian is an instrument by which God saves the world and keeps it from corruption and decay.

Salt can become insipid and savorless. In terms of discipleship, this means the loss of devotion, zest, and influence for Christ. Jesus urged his disciples to "have salt in yourselves, and be at peace with one another" (Mark 9:50). When salt becomes saltless its effectiveness is lost. Likewise, when the church loses her zeal for Christ and the gospel, there is no hope for the world.

Christian influence is also described in the symbol of light. Israel was to be "as a light to the nations" (Isa. 49:6), but she failed in her mission. Now the disciples are chosen to be the light to lead men to the truth. They are to bring the light of Christ to those "who sit in darkness and in the shadow of death" (Luke 1:79). They derive their light-giving quality from Christ who is "the light of the world" (John 8:12).

The symbol of light indicates the visible influence, whereas in the symbol of salt is described the silent influence of the Christian. He may put his "light under a bushel." The gospel can be hidden; influence for Christ can be negative. The "bushel" under which the light is hidden may be the fear of men, conformity to the world, sentimental humanitarianism, and other substitutes for the gospel.[10] Christians are to let their light shine "before men" in the world. This is a rebuke to the religious recluse, the hermit, and the monk who think that salvation is to be achieved by withdrawal from the world.

Christian Conduct (Matt. 5:17 to 7:12)

Matthew has a predilection to compare Christ with Moses. Christ on the Mount is portrayed as the "new law-giver" as over against Moses who gave the old law on Mount Sinai. Thus, the old righteousness of the law is contrasted with the new law of love.

The new criterion of conduct in contrast to the old (Matt. 5:17–20).—Righteousness as conformity to the will of God is the most comprehensive term for piety in both the Old and New Testaments. It is the sum of the attitudes and actions to be manifested toward God and man. In contrast to the old, the new righteousness of Christ "exceeds," is "over and above" it. Jesus declares to the disciples: "Unless your righteousness exceeds that of the scribes and Pharisees, you will never enter the kingdom of heaven" (Matt. 5:20). Here is the key verse of the sermon. Matthew seeks to show that the extraordinary righteousness of the kingdom is superior to that currently practiced by the Jews.

The new righteousness is superior to the old because Christ "fulfilled the law." He fulfilled the law in several ways. First, he simplified it by making love central, reducing the six hundred and thirteen laws of the Jews to the law of love to God and neighbor (Matt. 22:36–40). Sometimes he set aside the law in particular situations for the higher law of love to meet human needs, as in the case of healing on the sabbath (Matt. 12:1 ff.; Mark 2:23–28; Luke 6:1–5). He extended the law of love to neighbor to include enemies (Luke 10:25–37; Matt. 5:43–48). And, finally, he alone kept the law and exemplified it in his own life, thus revealing its deeper significance. Hence, Jesus did not come to abrogate the law, but to complete it—not to suspend, but to supplement it.

The new righteousness illustrated (Matt. 5:21 to 7:12).— Christ's new righteousness, then, is deeper and demands more than that taught and practiced by the Jews of his day. This fact is illustrated in the six antitheses contrasting the old righteousness and the new (Matt. 5:21–48).

The new righteousness of Christ demands more reverence for personality (5:21–26). The law says, "no murder" (Ex. 20:13). Jesus says, "no anger." In the old law, the act of murder exposes one to the judgment, that is, conviction and punishment by constituted authority of the local Sanhedrin, which is composed of twenty-three members. Jesus goes behind the act of murder to the angry passion which makes man liable to judgment, the judgment of God. Murders are the result of anger, and Jesus would prevent such by eliminating this passion in man. He goes on to warn against insulting one's fellow man. For example, to call a person "Raca" (a term of contempt equivalent to "empty-headed") is to be in danger of the council (Sanhedrin); and whosoever calls his fellow Christian a fool, a similar insult, is liable to the Gehenna of fire.

Such contempt for one's fellow Christian must be removed before one can truly worship God (Matt. 5:23–26). Mere performance of an act of worship does not atone for an offense against a brother. Duties to God never absolve one from duties to neighbor. To worship God acceptably, one must seek reconciliation with his brethren.

Again, the new ethic of Christ demands more respect for womanhood. The law says, "no adultery" (Ex. 20:14). Jesus says, "no lustful look" (5:27–30). He requires purity of thought as well as of action. The Jews tended to limit adultery to sexual intercourse of a man, married or unmarried, with a married or betrothed woman (Ex. 20:14; Deut. 5:18; Lev. 20:16). Jesus teaches that the lustful look is incipient adultery. The man our Lord has in mind, says Bishop Charles Gore,

must be supposed to have the deliberate intention to sin; he looks on the woman *in order to* excite his lust; he is only restrained from action (if it be so) by lack of opportunity or fear of consequences; in his will and intention he has already committed the act.[11]

Self-discipline will enable the individual to avoid sexual impurity. Spiritual surgery of the eye or the hand which provokes the sin is the remedy. For example, in present day society, this could well mean riddance of pornographic pictures, salacious literature, and the company of unchaste persons.

The new ethic of Christ demands more sanctity for the husband-wife relationship (5:31–32). The law says, "divorce on certain conditions" (Deut. 24:1 f.). Jesus says, "no divorce." But if Jesus allows no ground for divorce, how do we account for the "except it be for fornication" clause in Matthew 5:32? Some scholars hold that Matthew is watering down the absolute saying of Jesus on divorce to make it more acceptable to Jewish readers. This problem will be discussed more fully in a later chapter. At this point, suffice it to say that Jesus is affirming that Christian marriage is a sacred bond and that its purity must be upheld.

The new righteousness demands more truthfulness (Matt. 5:33–37). The old law says, "do not swear falsely" (Lev. 19:12). Jesus says, "swear not at all." The Mosaic law allowed oaths but forbade false swearing. In the time of Jesus, the Jews had developed a casuistical system of swearing which consisted of some oaths which were binding and others which were not binding (Matt. 23:16–22). For example, swearing by the temple was not binding but swearing by the gold of the temple was binding. In his statement, "swear not at all," Jesus sweeps away "the whole mechanics of swearing" and extends the obligation to tell the truth in all statements.[12] The Christian is to speak the truth in simplicity and to refrain from swearing "either by heaven or by earth or with any other oath" (James 5:12).

The new ethic of Christ demands non-retaliation (Matt. 5:38–42). The old law says, "an eye for an eye" (Ex. 21:23–25; Deut. 19:16–21). Jesus says, "no retaliation at all." Under the old law of blood revenge, the whole Hebrew tribe was involved and often the vengeance desired was nothing less than death. The *lex talionis,* the law of measure for measure, which goes back to the Code of Hammurabi ca. 1750 B.C., was introduced into Hebrew law and was designed to put a check on private revenge (Ex. 21:12–14; Deut. 19:21; Lev. 24:20). Adoption of this law limited vengeance and was actually a step up the moral ladder and a movement in the direction of mercy.

Jesus sets aside the *lex talionis* and teaches that all retaliation is wrong when he states the injunction, "resist not evil" (KJV). What does "evil" (*tō ponērōi*) mean in this context? The term is construed to be neuter by some scholars and masculine by others. The King James Version has the neuter, meaning evil in the abstract. The Revised Standard Version translates the word "one who is evil." This latter view seems to be the more acceptable translation. It is inconceivable that Jesus would suggest that no form of evil should be resisted. What he means is that the disciples should not "exact revenge for personal wrongs." [13] In other words, he is articulating the principle of non-retaliation in cases of personal relations. Verses 39 through 42 present graphic illustration of the principle and practice in terms of turning the cheek, the lawsuit, the second mile, and indiscriminate giving. These are moving pictures of the nonvindictive spirit in action.

The new righteousness-ethic revealed by Christ demands more love (5:43–48). The old law says, "love your neighbor" (Lev. 19:16–18). Jesus says, "love your enemies." There are two words for love in the New Testament: *philia,* which is love among friends—brotherly love; and *agape,* which is distinctive. Basically, *agape* has nothing to do with emotion or affection. It is primarily spontaneous good will which seeks the highest good of every man. We cannot always hold tender, affectionate feelings toward those who are personally hostile to us, but we can treat them justly and not return evil for evil. Certain characteristics of our neighbor we may dislike, but we can love him as a creature of God. Since the heavenly Father loves both the just and the unjust, the Christian is to be all inclusive in his love; he is to "be perfect, as [his] heavenly Father is perfect" (5:48). Here the righteousness-ethic reaches its supreme expression.

In Matthew 6:1–18, Jesus turns to the true motive of worship. Negatively, men are not to practice their piety or righteousness to be seen of men. Positively, the true motive of righteousness is to do everything for the glory of the Father "who is in heaven" (6:1). Thus, the new righteousness of the citizen of the kingdom is to glorify God. As Gore says: "God is its motive, God is its aim, God is its object; God, and nothing lower than God. No man is truly a citizen who is not in all his conduct and life looking directly God-ward." [14]

Jesus also speaks of the right practice of piety in terms of almsgiving, prayer, and fasting. In all three of these illustrations, he warns: "Do not parade your piety to win the approval of men." Thus, in giving alms, Jesus warns against being like the hypocrite, or "play actor," who sounds a trumpet to win the spectator's applause (6:2–4). In modern terms, this means "blowing one's own horn" when making a gift to a church or to some religious cause. The Greek word, *apechō,* translated "have their reward," was regularly used in commercial transactions in terms of receipts and meant "to receive in full." Thus the ostentatious giver has a piety which simmers down to a mere commercial transaction. His aim is to buy man's applause, and he gets it there and then. That is all the reward he is ever going to get, for the account is closed. "Let not your left hand know what your right hand does," is the principle which Jesus lays down for giving. That is to say, "don't give to be seen of men."

The true motive of righteousness is illustrated in prayer (6:5–15). In the act of prayer to God we are not to be "play actors," seeking applause. Those who pray to get the praises of men have their reward. As Gore says, "Every kind of conduct gets its reward on the plane of its motive." [15] True prayer consists of personal communion with God from the "inner closet." In so teaching Jesus does not condemn public worship (5:24; Luke 18:9–14); rather he condemns the effort to secure the approval of men.

In the "Lord's Prayer" (6:9–14), Jesus presents a pattern of prayer for his disciples. The prayer is divided into two parts: that which relates to God (9–10) and that which relates to man (11–13). It begins with "Our Father"—"Father of us" in the Greek. The Lord's Prayer, therefore, is primarily a social prayer to be prayed in private (6:6)!

The first petition is that God may be recognized in all this world as the Holy God: "Hallowed be thy name." God's name (that is, his nature and character) must be hallowed in thoughts, words, and deeds, as well as worship. "Father, glorify thy name," was also the petition of our Lord (John 12:28). In its fullest sense, the kingdom is still the future and is an object of prayer and hope; this petition is that the hope may be fulfilled (1 Cor. 15:28). "Thy will be done on earth as it is in heaven," is an extension and amplification of "Thy kingdom come." The kingdom of God is his will and his will is the kingdom of God. Wherever God's will is perfectly done as it is in heaven, there is the kingdom. For where God's will is done, there his sovereignty is made effective.

The new life in Christ is the doing of the divine will. It is the condition for becoming a follower of Christ (Mark 3:35); it is also a condition for entrance into the kingdom (Matt. 7:21). And those who do the will of God abide forever (1 John 2:17). The prayer that God's will may be done "on earth" means the whole earth which is to be reached with the message of God. Dr. W. O. Carver says that this prayer "has extensive reach, to the ends of the earth; and has intensive call to all energies and aspects of my own living." [16] It is not so much "a call to God to take us to heaven, but to bring heaven through us into the earth." [17] "As in heaven" is a standard which we on earth must seek to achieve. Note that the term "thy" is emphatic and refers to God's will, not to man's selfish interests.

The first three petitions of the Lord's Prayer relate to God, his name, his kingdom, and his will. The next three petitions of the prayer relate to man's necessities and needs. The fourth petition, therefore, is social in nature: "Give us this day our daily bread." The request is for bread, not a banquet. The exact meaning of the Greek word translated "daily" is unknown. It is interpreted variously to mean daily bread, tomorrow's bread, and heavenly bread. The weight of evidence seems to be in favor of the idea of bread necessary for existence during the coming day.

The fifth petition has to do with forgiveness: "Forgive us our debts, as we also have forgiven our debtors." When Christians ask God's forgiveness, they are to have already forgiven others. "Debts" is a Jewish figure for "sin" and is well illustrated in Matthew 18:23–25. Paul echoes this principle of forgiveness in Ephesians 4:32: "Be ye kind one to another, tenderhearted, forgiving one another, even as God for Christ's sake hath forgiven you" (KJV).

The final petition of the Lord's Prayer has to do with temptation and deliverance from evil. In the Bible, temptation may mean either "trial" or "enticement to evil." Here it appears to mean temptation which results in moral evil. Since God does not "lead us" into temptation to sin (James 1:13–14), the petition must be that God will help his children to avoid situations which involve moral peril where their resistance might break down. But the prayer is that if tempted one may not yield to evil. In his prayer in John 17:15, Jesus does not pray that the disciples be taken out of the world, but that they be kept from the evil one. Thus, this petition in the Lord's Prayer is not a plea that disciples never be tempted, but that they should not be brought *into* the evil of temptation. Augustine illustrates this point by the example of Joseph who was tempted to commit adultery by Potiphar's wife, but he was not brought into the sin of the temptation.[18]

The doxology (6:13b) does not appear in the more recent translations of the Bible, due to the fact that it was added in later manuscripts. However, it serves to end the prayer as it begins, with the thought of the sovereignty and glory of God.[19]

A third illustration of the true motive in worship is seen in the practice of fasting. Among the Jews, fasting was an outward sign of the inward experience of repentance. Pious Jews fasted twice a week (Luke 18:12). When fasting, the Pharisees put on a sad countenance and disfigured their faces in order to attract the attention of men. Thus they marred their appearance, that they might make an appearance! It was all done for self-glorification and praises of men. Jesus does not condemn fasting as a discipline but insists that it must be done in secret. Those who fast must be on guard, lest there should creep in a certain ostentation and hankering after the praise of men.

Thus far in the sermon, Jesus has described the Christian personality, influence, and the higher righteousness as it expresses itself in relation to the law and in true worship. Now (6:19–34) he shows that the new righteousness-ethic demands undivided allegiance to God and trust in his care. In the saying about treasuring up treasures on earth and the antithesis of treasuring up treasures in heaven, Jesus is teaching the proper attitude toward wealth. One's interest tends to be where he makes his investment. And, since Jesus does not deprive the human heart of its instinctive needs, he provides the heavenly treasure.[20] He makes available, in contrast to the worldly, a heavenly treasure which is a permanent possession. Matthew does not describe the nature of the heavenly treasure, but Mark (10:21) and Luke (12:33–34) indicate that it is gained by giving earthly possessions to the poor and needy (cf. Testament of Levi 13:5: "Do righteousness, my son, on earth, that you may have treasure in heaven.").

Jesus also illustrates the demand for absolute allegiance to himself with two small parables about the single eye and the single service (6:22–24). The "evil" or selfish eye cannot be focused on God and wealth at the same time. The single or generous eye which is focused on the glory of God illuminates the whole personality.

Absolute loyalty is also illustrated in the demand for singleness of service: "You cannot serve God and mammon." Allegiance to God must be above that of allegiance to mammon (personified, like the Greek Plutus). "But though we cannot serve God and money," says E. T. Thompson, "we can serve God with money." [21]

Jesus' teaching concerning anxiety is related to man's sense of economic insecurity (6:25–34). It is anxiety (*merima*) which stems from worldly care about what one shall eat, drink, and wear. Freedom from such anxious care comes from trustful assurance that the Father, who provides for the fowls and the flowers, shall much more care for his human children. Over-anxiety about earthly things, therefore, is unavailing, for one cannot by taking thought add one cubit to his stature; it is unnecessary, for God cares for those who trust him; and it is unbecoming to a Christian, since anxious care for material things is characteristic of the Gentiles. It should be noted that Jesus nowhere discounts forethought and carefulness about material things. He does teach, however, that material things must have a subordinate place in the kingdom of God.

When the Christian gives priority to the kingdom, the Father provides the necessities of life. "Seek first his kingdom and his righteousness, and all these things shall be yours as well" (6:33). Here Jesus is not disparaging the necessities of life. He is simply putting them in their proper place. The kingdom of God has priority.

Mutual treatment of others is the theme of Matthew 7:1–12. This section of the sermon is specifically concerned with conduct in terms of treatment of others. Here the righteousness-ethic is expressed in interpersonal relations. For one thing, the Christian is to avoid censorious judgment. The injunction is against censorious judgment and forbids all meddling, captious fault-finding, slander, and backbiting. This principle is strikingly illustrated in the small parable of the mote and the beam. The word rendered "mote" may be a splinter of wood. "Log" is a better translation than "beam." The parable teaches that it is absurd for a man to try to point out the sins of others when he does not see his own.

While the disciples are to be uncritical of others, they are not to be undiscriminating in their communication of God's truth. That which is "holy" is not to be given to the dogs, and "pearls" are not to be cast before swine, for they are incapable of receiving such precious things. Thus the disciples are to use moral discrimination in presenting the good news of the kingdom, turning away from those who cannot appreciate holy things to those who are receptive (cf. Matt. 10:13–14; 22:8–10).

How are Christians to acquire wisdom to exercise such moral discrimination and at the same time avoid censorious judgment? Christ says, "Ask, and it will be given you; seek and you will find; knock and it will be opened to you" (7:7 f.). When wisdom is needed it is to be sought from the Father's bounty, for he gives freely and upbraideth not (James 1:5, KJV).

This brings us to the Golden Rule (7:12; cf. Luke 6:31). Parallels to the Golden Rule can be found in both Jewish and Gentile sources. Tobit 4:15 states: "What thou hatest do to no man." Hillel, leader of the liberal group of Jews in the days of Jesus, put it, "What is unpleasant to thyself do not to thy neighbor. This is the whole law, and the rest is commentary upon it." Jesus' statement is distinctive in that it is positive in nature. William Barclay calls the Golden Rule the "Everest" of ethics and declares that there are no real Rabbinic parallels to this saying.[22] Jesus' concept of righteousness was not that of passivity but of positive action. Thus, the will of God is not simply refraining from wrongdoing, but engaging in right doing.

The Golden Rule is meant for Christians. Taken out of its context, it may be applied as a sanction for evil. For example, a child in the fourth grade in school received the answer to a question on a test. He justified this action by saying, "My classmate followed the Golden Rule when he told me the answer to the question I didn't know, because he would want me to tell *him* the answer to a question he didn't know." The Golden Rule must be interpreted in the light of the entire teaching of the Sermon on the Mount.

The test of character: discipline, dangers, and destiny (7:13–27).— Jesus concludes the Sermon on the Mount with some striking tests. There is the parable of the two ways—the way of life and death (cf. Deut. 11:26; Jer. 21:8). The broad way is the way of self-pleasing while the narrow way is that of self-discipline. But few are willing to pay the price of the disciplined and surrendered life.

There is the test of good and evil fruit. Jesus warns against the dangers of false teachers who present themselves as friends of the truth. The "wolves" come in sheep's clothing to deceive the sheep. They are not known by their beliefs, their interpretation of the Scriptures, their fidelity to creeds, but rather by their fruit— that is, their character and conduct.[23] Obviously, a good tree bears good fruit and a corrupt tree brings forth evil fruit.

There is the test of profession and practice. Jesus warns against profession without practice (7:21–23). Not everyone who says, "Lord, Lord, shall enter into the kingdom of heaven." Luke puts it: "Why do you call me 'Lord, Lord,' and not do what I tell you?" (Luke 6:46). Only those who do God's will enter into the kingdom of heaven. One may be thoroughly orthodox in doctrine but fail to translate this into Christian behavior. Thompson says that there is no error so dangerous as the common delusion that "doctrine can take the place of deeds, that orthodoxy (right beliefs) can substitute for orthopraxis (right conduct)." [24]

Finally, there is the test of obedience. Destiny is determined by response to the teaching of Jesus. He illustrates this truth with the story of the sensible man who builds his house on the rock and the stupid one who builds upon the sand. The "house" of Christian character is determined by response to God, the Great Architect, and the stones of truth in the sermon.

Conclusion (7:29).—When Jesus had finished the sayings of the Sermon on the Mount as reported by Matthew, the crowds were astonished at his teaching, "for he taught them as one who had authority, and not as their scribes." The scribes' authority was some great rabbi from whose writing they sought to give an exact verbal reproduction (Aboth 3:12). Christ's teaching carried its own authority, the truth of the thing itself.

Summary and Conclusion

Righteousness-ethics is the theme or thread which runs throughout the Sermon on the Mount. Christian character, influence, motive, conduct, and the tests of character are strikingly described. Obviously, the sermon is not a complete statement of the whole ethic of Jesus. His principle of service appears outside the sermon. There is no reference to his death and its significance for Christian ethics. Nor does he speak of the Holy Spirit, the church, the new covenant, baptism, and the Lord's Supper. But the sermon does contain the core of Jesus' moral teachings. It proclaims the pure will of God and gives radical examples of its expression in the Christian's attitudes and actions. Hence, here is the heart of Jesus' ethics which must be supplemented by the moral teachings in the larger New Testament.

References

1. See John Wick Bowman and Roland Tapp, *The Gospel from the Mount* (Philadelphia: Westminster Press, 1957), pp. 19–20.

2. Hans Windisch, *The Meaning of the Sermon on the Mount,* trans. S. M. Gilmour (Philadelphia: Westminster Press, 1951), pp. 63–64.

3. Charles Gore, *The Sermon on the Mount* (London: John Murray, 1928), p. 15.

4. A. M. Hunter, *A Pattern for Life* (Philadelphia: Westminster Press, 1953), p. 30.

5. Bowman and Tapp, *op. cit.*, p. 33.

6. William Barclay, *The Gospel of Matthew* (2nd ed.; Philadelphia: Westminster Press, 1958), I, 105.

7. Dietrich Bonhoeffer, *The Cost of Discipleship* (New York: Macmillan Co., 1949), p. 97.

8. See Paul Minear, *And Great Shall be Your Reward: The Origins of Christian Views of Salvation* (New Haven: Yale University Press, 1941), p. 48.

9. Lindsay Dewar, *An Outline of New Testament Ethics* (Philadelphia: Westminster Press, 1949), p. 49.

10. Bonhoeffer, *op. cit.*, p. 101.

11. Gore, *op. cit.*, pp. 64–65.

12. Hunter, *op. cit.*, p. 51.

13. L. H. Marshall, *The Challenge of New Testament Ethics* (New York: Macmillan Co., 1947), p. 116.

14. Gore, *op. cit.*, p. 105.

15. *Ibid.*, p. 111.

16. W. O. Carver, *Thou When Thou Prayest* (Nashville: Sunday School Board of the Southern Baptist Convention, 1928), p. 48.

17. *Ibid.*, p. 54.

18. "Sermon on the Mount," *The Nicene and Post-Nicene Fathers of the Christian Church,* ed. Philip Schaff (Grand Rapids: Wm. B. Eerdman's Publishing Co., 1956), VI, 44.

19. Hunter, *op. cit.*, p. 74.

20. Bonhoeffer, *op. cit.*, p. 151.

21. E. T. Thompson, *The Sermon on the Mount and Its Meaning for Today* (Richmond: John Knox Press, 1946), p. 108.

22. Barclay, *op. cit.*, pp. 276–277.

23. Thompson, *op. cit.*, p. 152.

24. *Ibid.*, p. 154.

Recommended Reading

AUGUSTINE, "Sermon on the Mount," *The Nicene and Post-Nicene Fathers of the Christian Church,* ed. PHILIP SCHAFF. Grand Rapids: Wm. B. Eerdman's Publishing Co., 1956, Vol. VI.

BONHOEFFER, DIETRICH, *The Cost of Discipleship.* New York: Macmillan Co., 1949.

BOWMAN, JOHN W. and TAPP, ROLAND, *The Gospel from the Mount.* Philadelphia: Westminster Press, 1957.

DIBELIUS, MARTIN, *The Sermon on the Mount*. New York: Charles
    Scribner's Sons, 1940.
HUNTER, A. M., *A Pattern for Life*. Philadelphia: Westminster Press,
    1953.
THOMPSON, ERNEST T., *The Sermon on the Mount and Its Meaning
    for Today*. Richmond: John Knox Press, 1953.
WINDISCH, HANS, *The Meaning of the Sermon on the Mount*. Phila-
    delphia: Westminster Press, 1951.

VIII
Ethics of Paul

Paul, the apostle, was the first great interpreter of "the mind of Christ" with reference to the ethical problems of early Christianity. The emergence of specific moral problems in the church at Corinth in particular, gave him the opportunity to apply to concrete issues the ethical ideals of Jesus. Thus what is ethically implicit in the Gospels becomes explicit in the Pauline epistles. Throughout his writings Paul is in harmony with the moral teaching of Jesus. As Professor C. A. A. Scott declares, "Paul may supplement but he never contradicts his Master." [1]

Theological Bases

Paul's ethical teachings are based squarely upon theological doctrines. One cannot understand his ethics without some knowledge of his theology, because both are part and parcel of the same reality. Obviously no adequate treatment of this relationship can be given in this study. However, instances can be presented which illustrate his use of theological doctrines to enforce ethical action.

In the first place, Paul's ethics is Christo-centric. The ground of the new life in Christ is oneness with him. Paul describes this experience as being "in Christ" (*en Christō*), an intimate relation of the Christian with his Lord (Rom. 16:3,9; 1 Cor. 1:30; 2 Cor. 5:17; Gal. 3:28; Col. 4:7; Phil. 4:1; 1 Thess. 3:8). This is a mystical relation, but not the kind which absorbs the person into nothingness. Rather, it is a practical mysticism which denotes belonging to Christ and behaving in mind and deed like him.[2] For to be "in Christ" is to take his attitude toward sin, to possess

69

a new ethical motive (Col. 3:1), and to have access to a new supply of moral power (Phil. 4:13).[3]

Secondly, Paul's ethic is an ethic of the Spirit. He conceives of the Spirit as none other than the Spirit of Christ. "The Lord is the Spirit (2 Cor. 3:17). Hence, in his concept of the Spirit, Paul makes the transition from the Jesus of history to the Jesus of personal experience. The Christian life becomes a life in the Spirit (Rom. 8). The Spirit produces the new being in Christ (Titus 3:5; Rom. 7:6), makes possible the knowledge of the will of God (1 Cor. 2:12–16), and produces the fruit of Christian character (Gal. 5:22). The Spirit also becomes the power of the new life in Christ, enabling the individual to live a life of moral victory (Eph. 3:16); and to "walk by the Spirit," not gratifying "the desires of the flesh" (Gal. 5:16).

Thirdly, Pauline ethics is grounded in the experience of repentance. While Paul rarely ever uses the term "repentance," the idea is dominant in his letters. "Renewing of the mind" is the equivalent of repentance in Paul's thought (Rom. 12:2). Karl Barth holds that this renewing of the mind (*nous*) or repentance "is the 'primary' ethical action upon which all secondary ethical conduct depends." [4] Repentance—the act of re-thinking or transformation of thought—Barth concludes, "is the key to the problem of ethics, for it is the place where the turning about takes place by which men are directed to a new behavior." [5]

Faith is closely related to Christian ethics in Pauline teaching. Faith is not mere intellectual assent to a creed, but self-commitment to Jesus Christ as Lord of life. So faith is an ethical act in which the whole personality is yielded in belief, trust, and obedience to the will of God in Christ. And while salvation is, by grace through faith, apart from works, faith is always productive of good works (Eph. 2:8–10). Indeed, "faith working through love" is at the very heart of Paul's ethics (Gal. 5:6).

Finally, the ethics of Paul is an ethics of the church. The sphere of the new life in Christ is the church, the fellowship of the redeemed. To be "in Christ" is to be in the church, the Body of Christ. The New Testament knows nothing of a Robinson Crusoe type of Christianity. As Dr. John A. Mackay says, "We be-

come related to Christ singly, but we cannot live in Christ soli-
tarily." [6]

Fellowship with Christ, therefore, leads necessarily to participation with other Christians. All share in the same Spirit and
partnership of the gospel of Christ (2 Cor. 13:14). When the
church is at worship, things are to be done for the good of all
concerned (1 Cor. 14:26). Gifts of the Spirit are to be used to
serve one another and the church as a whole (Rom. 12:5 f.;
2 Cor. 12:21, 27 f.). And Christians are to comfort one another
with the same comfort which they receive from Christ (2 Cor.
1:5–7).

Ethical Principles

Like Jesus, Paul presents no code of laws for the Christian life.
Rather, he lays down basic principles of behavior which the individual and the church can discover and apply in moral decision
and action.

Love is the chief moral principle of Paul's ethics. In his
thought, love—not law—is the indwelling and all-embracing
ethical force of the Christian life (Gal. 5:14). Love is "the more
excellent way" of life (1 Cor. 12:31). The practical proof of
Christianity is "faith working through love" (Gal. 5:6). This
means love for neighbor and especially for the brotherhood
(Gal. 6:10; Rom. 13:10). Love "builds up" (1 Cor. 8:1); it is
the "bond of perfection" (Col. 3:14) and "love never ends."
This is the basic truth of Paul's great ode to love in 1 Corinthians
13. Here love is seen as the greatest moral force in the world
which "reaches out beyond into the coming age." [7]

It must be noted that Paul's effort to replace law with love does
not mean that he abrogates the former or denies its value. Rather
he maintains that "the law is holy, and the commandment is holy
and just and good" (Rom. 7:12). Faith does not make void the
law but establishes it (Rom. 3:31). But Christ becomes the "end
of the law" as a means of salvation and righteousness. The new
"law of Christ," the law of love, becomes the guiding ethical force
(Gal. 6:2).

Paul is aware that the new freedom from the law may work out into license. Therefore he sets forth the limits of Christian liberty in terms of basic principles. This new freedom is to be used not as "an opportunity for the flesh" but to serve others through love (Gal. 5:13–17,25). Another limit is that of appropriateness: "All things are lawful," he says, "but not all things are helpful" ("fitting," "appropriate," or "profitable") to the good life (1 Cor. 10:23a). There is also the principle of constructiveness: " 'All things are lawful,' but not all things build up" the spiritual life (1 Cor. 10:23b). A decision must be made in the light of its constructiveness. And, finally, there is the limit of mastery: "All things are lawful for me," declares Paul, "but I will not be enslaved by anything" (1 Cor. 6:12b). When there is the question of moral action, the Christian must ask: "Is this an act of service in love? Is it appropriate? Is it the constructive thing to do? Will it enslave me?" These are the limits which Paul sets to Christian liberty.

The principle of righteousness is prominent in Pauline ethics. He constantly uses the idea of righteousness to describe God as the source of all that is good and just. While he does not think of righteousness as actually belonging to the believer, he does conceive it to be an objective norm which exercises authority over him.[8] Christ himself is the personification of righteousness (2 Cor. 6:15), and the kingdom is "righteousness and peace and joy in the Holy Spirit" (Rom. 14:17).

The Christian bears in his life the marks of righteousness. Through justification the believer is brought under the creative rule of the righteousness of God. He is set free from sin and becomes "the slave of righteousness" (Rom. 6:18). By wearing the "breastplate of righteousness," he is able to ward off the assaults of the evil one (Eph. 6:14). And it is Paul's prayer that the believer may abound in and be filled with "the fruits of righteousness."

Another principle of the Christian life in Paul's thought is the example of Christ. The *imitatio Christi* motif appears in several of his writings. The believer is to have the mind of Christ and to follow his example of humility (Phil. 2:5). Christ is to be imitated in his generosity and love (2 Cor. 8:9). Paul goes so far as to say, "Be imitators of me, as I am of Christ" (1 Cor. 11:1). An explanation of this principle is seen in 1 Thessalonians 1:6 where Paul states that these Christians had imitated Christ through himself and Timothy, because they welcomed the gospel in spite of much persecution.

Paul sums up the imitation principle by urging believers to live "according to Christ" (Col. 2:8). Obviously he does not mean that men should literally copy Jesus, but to emulate him in terms of spirit, inner ethical convictions, and concern for the propagation of the gospel.

Incentives of Christian Behavior

To stir up ethical responsibility among the early Christians, Paul appeals to various motives. One of these is the appeal to live in accordance with common standards of decency. As a minimum morality, they are to live up to the best ethical ideals of the period. Converts, therefore, are exhorted to maintain a decent family life, to work hard, to live quietly, to mind their own affairs, and so to live as to command the respect of those outside the Church (1 Thess. 4:1–12). Moreover, they are to pay their taxes and to show respect to civil authorities (Rom. 13:1 ff.).

On the negative side, Paul presents seven lists of sins which Christians are to avoid (Rom. 1:29–31; 1 Cor. 5:11; 6:9; 2 Cor. 12:20; Gal. 5:19–21; Eph. 4:31; 5:3–4; Col. 3:5–9).

These common sins or vices compose five groups. The first group includes sexual sins—fornication, uncleanness, lasciviousness, adultery, sodomy, effeminacy. Sins of selfishness—covetousness, extortion, insolence—comprise the second group. In the third group are sins of speech—whispering, backbiting, railing, boasting, shameful speaking, foolish talking, jesting, clamor. Bad personal relations—enmities, strife, factions, jealousies, wraths, divisions, heresies, envyings—and sins of drunkenness— drunken excesses, and revelings—are listed as groups four and five.

Christians who profess to live by the mature principle of love are not exempt from the common standards of decency. They are not injunctions for the morally immature alone. Life at the

level of love includes, and rises above, the best ethical requirements of the community.

Reason is another motif to which the Apostle appeals. Greek
thinkers, particularly the Stoics, considered reason as the ultimate
criterion of behavior. Though reason is by no means the supreme
motive to which he appeals, Paul is under the influence of this
Greek notion. For instance, he urges the Ephesians not to be
foolish and thoughtless but to "understand what the will of the
Lord is" (Eph. 5:17). Christian brethren are not to be childish
or immature in their thinking (1 Cor. 14:20). He reasons that
since Philemon is a Christian, then he should treat his runaway
slave, Onesimus, as a brother, for he is a Christian also (Philemon). And Paul asserts: "If then you have been raised with
Christ," it is logical that you should "seek the things that are
above" (Col. 3:1). All of these pleas are that Christians use
their intelligence in making moral decisions.

Desire to please God is another strong motive in Pauline ethics.
Christians are to make it their ambition to please God (2 Cor.
5:9), to behave as children of light, ever learning "what is
pleasing to the Lord" (Eph. 5:10). Preaching is not to please
men, but to "please God who tests our hearts" (1 Thess. 2:4;
4:1). Children of the flesh cannot please God (Rom. 8:8).

Paul pleads for a worthy walk on the part of Christians. To
"walk" in keeping with God's commands is a favorite symbol
for the good life in both the Old and New Testaments. Paul makes
use of the term "walk" in connection with the concept of calling.
Converts are to lead a life worthy of the calling: walking in love,
light, and wisdom (Eph. 4:1 ff.; 5:8,15). They are not to walk
as other Gentiles—in futility of mind, hardness of heart, and
uncleanness (Eph. 4:17–19). Hence, the old nature, characterized by lying, anger, stealing, evil talk, and malice, must be put
off (Eph. 4:25–31a). In contrast to the old way of life, they are
to "be kind to one another, tenderhearted, forgiving one another,
as God in Christ forgave you" (verse 32).

Sensitivity to the needs of the weaker brother is another appeal
of the Apostle. Sometimes those stronger in the faith should
forego their individual rights so that the weaker brother's con-

science may not be weakened or offended (1 Cor. 8:1–13). Living participation in the troubles of those in need calls for active help. Since Hebrew Christians have shared their spiritual blessings with Gentile converts, it is the latter's duty to help the mother church by contributing material things to aid them (Rom. 15: 26–27). Thus, for Paul the collection of money is more than a mere financial affair. Rather, it is a deep expression of fellowship between Jewish and Gentile churches (1 Cor. 16:1–4). Actually Paul is concerned with developing an ecumenical fellowship which recognizes a kinship with all Christians who make up the Body of Christ.

Eschatology and ethics are intertwined in Pauline ethics. For instance, Paul does not hesitate to appeal to fear of the coming wrath of God. He declares that wicked men store up for themselves wrath on the day when God's righteous judgment will be revealed (Rom. 2:5). This "day of wrath" hovers like a cloud over all ungodliness and unrighteousness of men who delude themselves into thinking that they can mock or sneer at God. Retribution is sure, for whatever a man sows he will reap (Gal. 6:7). The wages of sin is death (Rom. 6:23).

Every Christian must appear before the "judgment seat" (a Greek term meaning "award-throne" which was used in Olympian games) of Christ to receive his due, good or evil, according to what he has done in the body (2 Cor. 5:10). Hence, the appearance of Christians before the judgment seat is more for the purpose of awards than judgment (cf. parable of the talents in Matt. 25:14 ff.). For they have already passed from under condemnation (Rom. 8:1). Their desire should be to appear blameless on the day of the Lord (1 Cor. 1:8). To do so, they must assume an attitude of soberness and self-discipline (1 Thess. 5:4–11).

Finally, Paul appeals to the idea of the perfect personality, the mature person, as an incentive to Christian living. When the elements of Christian character, as Paul describes them, are put together, we have a mosaic of the mature person. These traits of the mature man are seen in Paul's lists of virtues which reflect the Greek influence, particularly the Stoic view of virtue. Paul exhorts: "Whatever is true, whatever is honorable, whatever is just, whatever is pure, whatever is lovely, whatever is gracious, if there is any excellence, if there is anything worthy of praise, think about these things" (Phil. 4:8). The perfect personality also includes the fruit of light: the good, the right, and the true (Eph. 5:9), and the fruit of the Spirit: love, joy, peace, patience, kindness, goodness, fidelity, gentleness, and self-control (Gal. 5:22 f.). This kind of character, in contrast to the Greek view, is formed not merely by reason, moderation, and virtuous acts, but by the indwelling of the Spirit.

The mature person conducts himself with dignity and grace in his relations with non-Christians. His speech is gracious and he knows how to answer every man who puts a question to him about his faith (Col. 4:5–6). Thus the Christian life should be an example of "good breeding" and present itself in the world in a "winning manner." [9] Everything is to be done decently and in order (1 Cor. 14:40).

These ideals of the perfect personality motif are rooted in Paul's own life and reflect his aristocratic rearing. Hence, Paul's ethics is that of a moral aristocracy, a *noblesse oblige*, and much of his teaching and preaching is the working out of the ethical meaning of this motif. Thus he proclaims Christ, "warning every man and teaching every man in all wisdom, that we may present every man mature in Christ" (Col. 1:28).

Pauline Realism

A genuine realism pervades Paul's conception of man and his moral possibilities. Pauline anthropology, in contrast to the Greek dualistic view of man, conceives the human person in his entirety: body, soul, and intellect. So closely is the soul aligned with man's creature-like nature, that Paul can speak of "soul-like-bodies" (*sōma psuchikon*, 1 Cor. 15:44). Man, therefore, is a basic unity who is not to be arbitrarily divided into soul and body.

Paul speaks of the unregenerate man as the "natural man." As natural man he is incapable of understanding spiritual things, for such truth is spiritually discerned (1 Cor. 2:14). Natural man must, therefore, become a "new creature" in Christ by the transforming power of the Spirit. This new spiritual life is not a mere improvement of the natural life. To be "in Christ" is to become a new creation altogether, in opposition to the previous old spiritual and moral condition. "Therefore, if any one is in Christ, he is a new creation; the old has passed away, behold, the new has come. All this is from God" (2 Cor. 5:17–18).

No detailed explanation of the origin of sin in man and the world is given by the Apostle. He simply says that "by one man sin came into the world," that is, by the act of Adam. Nor does he answer the question as to how sin passes from Adam to all men. He is satisfied with the assumption that "all have sinned" (Rom. 3:23) and, therefore, sin is universal (Rom. 3:10). In this condition, man is confronted with God's law which he is incapable of fulfilling. The law can only lead man to Christ, the hope of salvation (Gal. 3:24).

As for the seat of sin, Paul tends to locate it in the "flesh" (*sarx,* Rom. 7:17–20). By flesh he does not mean body (*sōma*), but the natural man as a whole, the total person without God and the Spirit. Flesh and spirit are in constant conflict in man (Gal. 5:17*b*). Only by living habitually in the Spirit can man avoid gratifying the cravings of the flesh (Gal. 5:16). This constant struggle helps to explain why man does not always achieve the highest good.

For all of his devotion to Christ, Paul never assumes absolute perfection for himself. He frankly admits that he has not achieved this high goal (Phil. 3:12 ff.). Nevertheless he is on the road to perfection, striving to win the prize to which God in Christ is calling him onward and upward. The high ideals of the gospel can only be approximated and this is never achieved automatically, but in constant conformity to the will of God in Christ.

In conclusion, Paul articulates in various ways the basic principles of Christian ethics, seeking to motivate men to embody them in their own lives. His principles of ethics, appeals for Christian action, and his view of man are realistic and, therefore, valid and permanent. And while these views were expressed in the first century of the church, they nevertheless transcend every age and belong to all centuries.

References

1. C. A. A. Scott, *New Testament Ethics* (Cambridge: University Press, 1936), p. 75.
2. F. C. Porter, *The Mind of Christ in Paul* (New York: Charles Scribner's Sons, 1930), pp. 283 f.
3. James S. Stewart, *A Man in Christ* (New York: Harper & Bros., n.d.), pp. 196 ff.
4. Karl Barth, *The Epistle to the Romans,* translated from the sixth edition by E. C. Hoskyns (London: Cumberlege, Oxford University Press, 1933), p. 436.
5. *Ibid.*
6. John A. Mackay, *God's Order: The Ephesian Letter and This Present Time* (New York: Macmillan Company, 1953), p. 117.
7. "Love," *Bible Key Words from Gerhard Kittel's Theologisches Wörterbuch Zum Neuen Testament.* Translated and edited by J. R. Coates (New York: Harper & Bros., 1951), p. 59.
8. Gottfried Quell and Gottlob Schrenk, "Righteousness," in *ibid.,* p. 53.
9. Johannes Weiss, *Earliest Christianity: A History of the Period A.D. 30–150* (New York: Harper Torchbooks, 1959), II, 568.

Recommended Reading

ALEXANDER, A. B. D., *The Ethics of Paul.* Glasgow: J. Maclehose and Sons, 1910.

DODD, C. H., *The Meaning of Paul for Today.* London: George Allen and Unwin, Limited, 1920.

ENSLIN, MORTON SCOTT, *The Ethics of Paul.* New York: Harper & Bros., 1930.

HUNTER, A. M., *Interpreting Paul's Gospel.* London: S.C.M. Press, 1955.

MACKAY, JOHN A., *God's Order: The Ephesian Letter and This Present Time.* New York: Macmillan Company, 1953.

STEWART, JAMES S., *A Man In Christ.* London: Hodder & Stoughton, 1935.

IX

Ethics of Other New Testament Writings

Ethical emphases in the teaching of Jesus appear not only in Paul's writings, but also in works of other writers of the New Testament. While no distinctively new note is struck in these materials, they do serve to make more explicit the basic ethical principles of Jesus and Paul. For example, the writings of John are a commentary on the primacy of love in the Synoptic Gospels and in Paul. James' epistle is an echo of the Sermon on the Mount. Hebrews, 1 and 2 Peter, and Jude also contain relevant moral principles as applied to certain problems. And the book of Acts has much to contribute to our understanding of the Holy Spirit in relation to moral action.

The Johannine Corpus

In John's writings, the commandment of love is supreme, being "repeated and set before the reader with magnificent monotony." [1] A "new commandment" to love as Christ loves appears in John 13:34: "A new commandment I give to you, that you love one another; even as I have loved you, that you also love one another." This commandment contains a new dimension —"as I have loved you." Christ himself becomes the criterion of all Christian behavior. The Jewish commandment to love one's neighbor is qualified by love of self. To love as Christ loves is to make love all-embracing, unconditional, redemptive, and selfless. It thus makes more explicit what is involved in love of neighbor

79

in thought and deed. Practice of this new commandment is proof of genuine discipleship (John 13:35).

John's first epistle is a brief commentary on the inseparability of love to God and to one's neighbor. The ground of the Christian life consists of being begotten of God and living in fellowship with him (3:9; 5:18). Conditions of fellowship with God are walking in the light, confession of sin, and obedience to his commandments. This involves the *imitatio Christi* motif for moral behavior (1 John 2:6,29; 3:3). Tests of the Christian life are righteousness (2:29), brotherly love (3:11–24), and belief in Jesus Christ as the Son of God (5:1–12). Love is not merely theoretical but expresses itself in meeting human need: "But if any one has the world's goods and sees his brother in need, yet closes his heart against him, how does God's love abide in him? Little children, let us not love in word or speech but in deed and in truth" (3:17–18).

Likewise, John's second epistle appeals for the demonstration of love in conduct. One is to "pass his life in love" (verse 6, Montgomery's translation). In his third epistle, John stresses love in terms of doing the truth (3–4) and practicing hospitality to missionaries (5–8). He issues a warning against an ambitious person, Diotrephes, who "likes to put himself first" (verse 9). And he urges Christians to "imitate good," concluding that: "He who does good is of God; he who does evil has not seen God" (verse 11).

The ethical content of John's apocalypse has been sadly neglected. The book too frequently has been regarded as purely prophetic (foretelling), devoid of any ethical teaching. The fact that the book is a summary of "Christian politics" is usually overlooked.[2] In his discussion of Revelation 13, Oscar Cullmann has convincingly shown that the first beast emerging from the sea represents the Roman totalitarian state and that the second beast or "false prophet" is the minister of false propaganda which is essential to the existence of any tyrannical government.[3] The fundamental message of the revelation, therefore, is that of the ultimate triumph of Christ, the Lamb, over the beast, the totalitarian state. John, the apostle, describes this conflict between Christ and Caesar from a concentration camp on the Isle of Patmos. From this lonely isle he envisions the triumph of Christ over all his earthly enemies.

Thus the basic principle of the sovereignty of Christ which lies behind the apocalyptic symbols bears a message of encouragement for our age. Gripped by the conviction that "the Lord God Omnipotent reigneth" over all powers, the suffering church will triumph under every existing tyrannical power.

Epistle to the Hebrews

Loyalty and staying power are the central ethical appeals of the book of Hebrews. Those who are about to slip back into the ways of Judaism are reminded that Christianity is the perfect and final faith. For, in the cross, Christ's sacrifice secures access to God which Judaism could only shadow and symbolize. Christ is greater than the angels (chs. 1–2); he is superior to Moses (3:1–6); he belongs to a higher order of the priesthood (ch. 7). Christ is, therefore, the ideal high priest who offers the perfect sacrifice for sin (9:11–28). The argument culminates with proof of the futility of Jewish sacrifices, which can never make perfect those who draw near, and the crucified, yet living, Christ as man's only hope of redemption (10:1–18).

Among the other virtues emphasized in Hebrews are faith, patience, and perseverance (6:12; 12:1–2). Also, love as the ground of good deeds is stressed: "For God is not so unjust as to overlook your work and the love which you showed for his sake in serving the saints" (6:10). Christians are to provoke one another "to love and good works" (10:24). Brotherliness in all relations is urged: "Let brotherly love continue" (13:1). Fearlessness and boldness are to characterize the Christian (4:16; 10:19; 13:6). Fornication and adultery are condemned, and the honorable nature of marriage commended (13:4). Life is to be free from "besetting sins," including the love of money (12:1–2; 13:5). The imitation of Christ motif appears in chapter 12, verse 2, where the Christian is taught to look to Jesus, "the pioneer and perfecter of our faith, who for the joy that was set before him endured the cross."

Epistle of James

James' letter is largely an ethical tract. It echoes in a remarkable way the ethics of the Sermon on the Mount.[4] The purpose of the letter is to explain the basic connection between faith and works. "Pure religion," as it is expressed in outward acts, consists in caring for the needy and keeping oneself from the contamination of the world. As the author puts it: "Religion that is pure and undefiled before God and the Father is this: to visit orphans and widows in their affliction, and to keep oneself unstained from the world" (1:27). Here theology and ethics are inseparably bound together, being rooted in God the Father and manifested in all areas of the Christian life.

Faith's practical meaning is seen in several injunctions. There is the warning against social snobbery and class distinctions in the churches (2:1–13). The "royal law" of love involves sharing of possessions with those in need (2:8,14–16) and the control of the tongue (3:1 ff.). Teachers who are wise manifest their faith in a good life (3:13). False wisdom produces bitter jealousy, rivalry, and selfish ambition. False wisdom is earthly, sensual, and demonic. True wisdom is heavenly with a sevenfold nature (3:17–18). Causal factors in war are unfulfilled lust and covetousness (4:1 ff.). Evil-speaking of one's neighbor is rebuked, for God who gave the law is the final judge (4:11–12).

James goes on to denounce social injustices of the rich who gain their goods through oppression (5:1 ff.). He speaks specifically of those who keep back, by fraud, just and lawful wages from workers. Cries and appeals of the employees have fallen on deaf ears, but the God of hosts hears and will establish judgment. So serious is the act of defrauding the workers that the Lord regards it as a form of murder (James 5:6)!

Turning from the oppressors to the oppressed, James urges the reclamation of sinners "until the coming of the Lord."

First Epistle of Peter

The purpose of this epistle is twofold: to strengthen the Christians in persecution and to clarify the true principles of Christian living. Peter's ethical thought is an extension and application of the ethical teaching of his Lord.[5] The Apostle begins with an ascription of praise to God for the blessings of the redeemed (1:3–12). Then he follows logically with a call to holy living in all conduct and points up the need for spiritual growth (1:13 to 2:10). Christians are to be characterized by purity of life because God is holy (1:13–16); for they have been redeemed by Christ at infinite cost (1:18–21); and they have been born anew (1:22–25). The church, with Christ as the foundation stone, becomes the New Israel, a chosen race, a royal priesthood, a holy nation, God's own people, to declare the wonderful deeds of Christ (2:4–10).

The *imitatio Christi* motif is prominent throughout the letter (1:16; 2:21–25; 4:1). Christians are to "follow in his steps" (2:21). This imitation principle and that of submission are prominent ones which ought to govern the Christian in relation to others. Good conduct among unbelievers is to be maintained, so that if Christians are slandered, the slanderers by evidence of the believer's good deeds will be compelled to glorify God (2:11–12).

The principle of submission is thus stated: "Be subject for the Lord's sake to every human institution . . ." (1 Peter 2:13a), and is illustrated in several relationships. Believers are to be in submission to heads of government (2:13–17). This cannot mean blind obedience to the state, because Peter himself declares that the Christian must obey God rather than man when obedience to rulers conflicts with duty to God (Acts 5:29). Again, the principle is illustrated in the slave-master relationship. Slaves are to be submissive to their masters, even though it means suffering unjustly (2:18 ff.). But it should be noted that the "slaves" are household-servants and not members of a particular social class.[6] Hence, they are not bondslaves such as those of work gangs under cruel taskmasters. They are to render faithful service in the fear of God, for this is well-pleasing to him.

Wives also are to be submissive to their husbands (3:1–6). By so doing they may win unbelieving husbands to Christ by their good lives. Husbands are to live with their wives in practical understanding in all relationships, giving them due honor. And, finally, the younger is to be in subjection to the elders (5:5), that is, to the spiritual guides of the church, giving them due respect and heeding their counsel.

The principle of submission may be a bit unsavory to the modern democratic mentality. But it should be noted that submission in the above instances is a voluntary act and not a political or social law. It is a religious principle by which we serve God: "For it is the will of God that by doing right your good and honest lives should stop the ignorant charges and criticisms of foolish people" (author's paraphrase, 2:15). Moreover, submission is a reciprocal relationship, binding upon all Christians: rulers, slaves, masters, husbands, wives, youth, and elders (5:5; cf. Gal. 5:13; Eph. 5:21 ff.; 6:1–9; Titus 3:1; Philemon 15–17).

In the Christian community, life is to be characterized by unity of spirit, sympathy, love of the brethren, tenderheartedness and humble-mindedness. An echo of the Sermon on the Mount is heard in the injunction: "Do not return evil for evil or reviling for reviling; but on the contrary bless, for to this you have been called, that you may obtain a blessing" (3:9). In view of the coming crisis, Christians are to keep sane and sober, use their gifts for the edification of others, and be patient, humble, and trustful in persecution (4:7 to 5:10).

Second Epistle of Peter

The writer's primary concern in this epistle is for the maintenance of the true faith and high standards of Christian morality which are being threatened by false teachers. Affirming the divine character of the Christian life, he goes on to present a list of virtues which Christians are to add to their faith. Thus, he urges that they make every effort in exercising their faith to develop virtue (moral energy and excellence), knowledge (practical wisdom), self-control (restraint of sensual impulses), steadfastness (endurance to hold out against evil), godliness (genuine piety), brotherly affection, and love (1:5–11). These ideals are in direct contrast to the seven "virtues" of ordinary church members as defined by a noted modern dramatist in terms of respectability, childishness, mental timidity, dullness, sentimentality, censoriousness, and depression of spirits.[7]

Christians are to beware of false teachers who separate Christian faith and ethics (ch. 2). Such teachers can be detected by the marks they bear. They introduce destructive heresies, deny the Lord, practice immoral ways, discrediting "the way of truth" in the eyes of the world (2:1–2). In their covetousness they exploit the people by cunning and false arguments. Irrational animals, they are self-willed, self-loving, lustful, sensual creatures (2:10–16). Obviously the kind of heresy described is that of antinomianism, the teaching that, under grace, the moral law is not relevant since faith alone is sufficient for salvation. Such teachers shall perish in their own corruption. In their destroying they shall be destroyed (2:12).

Chapter 3 deals with the coming day of the Lord. The author declares: "But the day of the Lord will come like a thief, and then the heavens will pass away with a loud noise, and the elements will be dissolved with fire, and the earth and the works that are upon it will be burned up" (3:10). In light of the coming of Christ, Christians are to be characterized by holy living, a vision of a new heaven and a new earth, steadfastness in the faith, and continuous growth in the grace and knowledge of Jesus Christ (chapter 3).

Epistle of Jude

This small letter appears to be addressed to Jewish Christians who are using their freedom from the law as an occasion for unethical living. Originally the author intended to write a treatise on "our common salvation" (v. 3). Learning of false teachers, he writes an earnest appeal urging his readers to strive for the true standards of the faith "once for all delivered to the saints" (v. 3). These false teachers bear the same marks as those described in 2 Peter, and apparently are antinomians. They are grumblers, malcontents, lustful, loud-mouthed boasters, flattering people when they think it will bring them advantage (v. 16). Holy living is the best testimony to the true faith. Christians, therefore, are urged to build themselves up in the faith, to pray in the

Spirit, to keep themselves in the love of God, and to work for the spiritual and moral recovery of others (vv. 20 ff.).

Such is the ethical content of the Johannine corpus, Hebrews, James, 1 and 2 Peter, and Jude. Most of this ethical material, in principle, is found in Jesus and Paul. Yet to be considered is the ethical role of the Holy Spirit. In the next chapter this neglected aspect of Christian morality will be examined.

References

1. Ethelbert Stauffer, "Love," *Bible Key Words from Gerhard Kittel's Theologisches Wörterbuch Zum Neuen Testament.* Translated and edited by J. R. Coates (New York: Harper & Bros., 1951), p. 63.

2. See F. D. Maurice, *Lectures on the Apocalypse* (London: Macmillan Co., 1895), Lecture XIII.

3. Oscar Cullmann, *The State in the New Testament* (New York: Charles Scribner's Sons, 1956), p. 76.

4. Cf. 1:12 and 20 with Matthew 5:11,22; 1:22 with 7:24-25; 2:5 with 5:3; 2:8 with 7:12; 2:10 with 5:19; 2:13 with 5:7; 2:18 with 7:16 ff.; 3:12 with 7:16; 4:4*b* with 6:24; 4:11 ff. with 7:1-5; 5:10 with 5:12; 5:11 with 5:10 and 5:12 with 5:34-37.

5. Cf. 1:13-Luke 12:35; 2:12-Matthew 5:16; 3:9-Luke 6:28; 3:14-Matthew 5:10; 4:5-Matthew 12:36; 4:14-Matthew 5:11; 5:6-Luke 14:11; 5:7-Matthew 6:25 ff.

6. E. G. Selwyn, *The First Epistle of St. Peter* (London: Macmillan Co., 1946), p. 175.

7. Dorothy L. Sayers, *Creed or Chaos* (London: Methuen & Co., 1947), p. 23.

Recommended Reading

DEWAR, LINDSAY, *An Outline of New Testament Ethics.* Philadelphia: Westminster Press, 1949, Chapters 4–5.

MAURICE, F. D., *The Epistles of Saint John: A Series of Lectures on Christian Ethics.* London: Macmillan Co., 1893.

ROBERTSON, A. T., *Some Practical and Social Aspects of Christianity: The Wisdom of James.* New York: Hodder & Stoughton, 1915.

STEVENS, GEORGE B., *The Theology of the New Testament.* New York: Charles Scribner's Sons, 1899, Parts 5–7.

X

Ethics of the Holy Spirit

One of the central, yet neglected, doctrines in Christian ethics is that of the Holy Spirit. This is true in spite of the fact that the Spirit's role in Christian morality contributes to its unique and distinct nature. "The vision of God's holy love, seen through the windows of Christ's mind and mediated by his Spirit," says F. R. Barry, "is the differentia of the Christian ethic." [1] Disregard for this relation of the Spirit to morality has led not only to the loss of the distinctiveness of the Christian ethic but also to the impoverishment of our understanding of its meaning.

Reasons for neglect of the Spirit's function in Christian morality are not difficult to ascertain. Any suggestion of being "spirit-filled" or "spirit-led" is often identified with ecstatic and emotional sectarian groups. It is sometimes assumed that the ethical teaching of the Gospels, especially that of the Sermon on the Mount and the Great Commandment, is the whole of Christian ethics. Professor T. W. Manson, a leading New Testament scholar, declares that the two commandments—love of God and neighbor—"are sufficient without any supplement whatever, as a complete guide to anyone who wishes to live thereby." [2] Moreover, the Spirit in ethics is neglected because he is to be experienced and not merely an empirical factor for intellectual consideration. And finally, the doctrine of the Spirit is beset by difficulties which baffle us. Since the Spirit involves the doctrine of the Trinity and is referred to in varied ways in the Scriptures, we see this teaching "through a glass darkly." Perhaps some insight may come by focusing attention upon the moral nature and function of the Holy Spirit.

87

The Ethical Nature of the Holy Spirit

Early Old Testament literature describes the divine Spirit as a Power, not a Person, which has little to do with ethical ideas. Rather, the Spirit is simply "the power that lay behind abnormal action, and ethical interests which that action might promote are not considered." [3] The Spirit is active in creation (Gen. 1:1 ff.) and imparts life to man (Gen. 2:7). Beyond creation the Spirit holds together that which has been created and engages further in creation. Daily the world is renewed when God sends forth his Spirit. Withdrawal of his Spirit results in the destruction of life (Psalm 104:29–30). Since the creation, then, the Spirit has been the source of all life upon earth as "the life-giving Spirit" (1 Cor. 15:45). The impulse moving the whole universe forward is the Spirit of the living God.

In the Old Testament the Spirit is also associated with charismatic gifts of prophecy (1 Sam. 10:6; Isa. 61:1; Mic. 3:8). Unusual physical strength is conferred by the Spirit upon Samson (Judg. 14:6), wisdom and skill upon Bezalel (Ex. 31:3–5), leadership in war upon Gideon (Judg. 6:34). The Spirit also appears to produce evil results (1 Sam. 19:9), and to transport prophets from one place to another (1 Kings 18:12). The Messiah is to be anointed by the Spirit (Isa. 11:1–5), and Joel predicts the outpouring of the Spirit upon all people (Joel 2:28–29).

Down to the Exilic period, the dominant idea of the Spirit was amoral. From the Exilic and post-Exilic periods forward, the Spirit was viewed increasingly as performing a moral role. [4] As long as the Hebrews held nonethical views of God, naturally their concept of the Spirit was nonethical. But with the rise of the eighth-century prophets and the concept of the righteousness of God, "the distinction between good and bad was perforce gradually extended to all spheres of conduct." [5]

In the New Testament the concept of the Holy Spirit becomes both personal and ethical. The Synoptic Gospels describe the work of the Spirit in association with Jesus, his conception (Matt. 1 and Luke 1), his baptism (Mark 1:10), and his ministry

(Matt. 12:28). Hence, the Spirit is still viewed as somewhat impersonal. In the Fourth Gospel the qualities of personality are definitely ascribed to the Spirit (see John 14:26; 16:13 f., where the masculine pronoun *ekeinos* is applied to the Spirit). The Spirit is the paraclete, the teacher, the counselor—all of which invests him with the essential attributes of personality.[6]

The chief personage in the Acts is neither Peter nor Paul, but the Spirit who makes for the addition of members to the church (9:31), who gives guidance in decisions effecting harmony (15:28), and who sets aside and directs missionaries (4:8; 6:10; 8:29; 10:19; 13:2–4; 20:22). So prominent is the Spirit in Acts that this work is frequently called "The Acts of the Holy Spirit."

In the Epistles, the Spirit becomes the abiding moral guide and sustainer of the Christian life. Only Philemon, 2 and 3 John fail to mention the Holy Spirit. In his writings, Paul shows a close connection between Christ and the Spirit. He declares that the "Lord is the Spirit" (2 Cor. 3:17). A. M. Hunter points out that, in bringing Christ and the Spirit close together, Paul helps to personalize the Spirit and to ethicize his action.[7] He further observes:

By "playing-down" the less wholesome evidences of the Spirit, he [Paul] helped to *moralize* men's thinking about it. By his conception of the Spirit as "leading," "witnessing" and "pleading" he helped to *personalize* their thought about it. And by linking the Spirit with the living Christ, he helped to *christianize* their thoughts.[8]

We conclude that since the "Lord is the Spirit," the Spirit is of the same nature with the Father and the Son. He is God and Christ, active in the hearts of men—regenerating, counseling, and energizing. And, just as sin is an offense to the Father and the Son, so it is to the Spirit (Acts 5:3). He is grieved by sins of disciples (Eph. 4:30), including sins against the body, which is "a temple of the Holy Spirit" (1 Cor. 6:19–20).

The Ethical Role of the Holy Spirit

The Holy Spirit is God in action. His moral functions are manifold. The Christian's moral life is guided and sustained by the Spirit. He is the energizer and enabler of Christian moral living. Without his work Christian ethics is incomplete and impractical.

The Spirit and the Christian's Moral Life

The Spirit convicts and convinces the world of sin, righteousness, and judgment (John 16:8). He actualizes the new birth (Titus 3:5), by which we become "new creations" in Christ (2 Cor. 5:17). He enables the Christian to live in fellowship with the Father and the faithful (Rom. 8:14–17; Phil. 1:27). Christian sonship is assured by the Spirit who bears "witness with our spirits that we are the children of God" (Rom. 8:16). He, therefore, does not destroy our spirits or their freedom, but rather establishes them. And it is in this sphere of the human spirit that "the ethical work of the Holy Spirit is carried forward." [9]

The Spirit, then, is the Power-Personality dwelling within the Christian, empowering him for action (1 Cor. 6:19–20). In other words, the Christian is indwelt by the divine *Dunamis* from whom he draws "miraculous stores of moral power." [10] It is the function of the Spirit to lay hold of our nature and inwardly change it, "making it susceptible of a higher moral life." [11] Without this indwelling and energizing Spirit, Christian principles would be impotent and irrelevant.

The Spirit is the source of all gifts and ministries distributed among Christians for the common good of the community (1 Cor. 12:1–31; cf. 1 Peter 4:10). Different gifts are imparted to each, but they are to be used for the profit of the whole congregation. Among these gifts is the power to speak wisdom, to utter knowledge, to express wonder-working faith, to heal, to work miracles, to prophesy, to distinguish between true and false spirits, to speak in various tongues, and to interpret various tongues. All of these abilities are inspired by the same Spirit who apportions to each as he chooses.

The Spirit enables the Christian to develop moral character. The fruit of the Spirit is defined by Paul in ethical terms: love, joy, peace, patience, kindness, goodness, faithfulness, gentleness, and self-control (Gal. 5:22). (Note that the term "fruit" is in the singular to denote the unity of Christian morality.) Thus the work of the Spirit is morality, not magic; ethics, not emotionalism.

Converts are strengthened in the inner man with the power of the Spirit (Eph. 3:16), and by this same power abound in hope (Rom. 15:13). The Spirit delivers them from sin (Rom. 8:2) and enables them to be victorious in the battle with evil (Gal. 5:16; Eph. 6:17). Worldwide witnessing is possible only through the power of the Spirit (Acts 1:8). This is the same divine power which raised Christ from the dead and which made effective Paul's preaching ministry (Rom. 1:4; 15:18 f.; 1 Cor. 2:4; 2 Cor. 13:4; 1 Thess. 1:5).

It is obvious that the Holy Spirit supersedes the law as a power for righteousness in the Christian, becoming "a living energy instead of a dead mechanism of a written code." [12] By the power of the Spirit "we serve not under the old written code but in the new life of the Spirit" (Rom. 7:6). Life in the Spirit, therefore, has "an inwardness, a vitality, a personal quality, a moral responsibility," which sets it apart from magic.[13] For man, the law was impossible; but the Spirit makes it possible for him "to overcome the lower nature and follow out the will of God." [14]

The Spirit and the Church's Moral Life

The church as well as the individual is the temple of the Spirit (1 Cor. 3:16). He indwells the church and acts in and through her. The ethical action of the Spirit in the church is seen in several instances. A permanent result of Pentecost was the emergence of a fellowship, a community of sharing (*hē koinōnia*). There was a sense of oneness among the disciples (Acts 4:32) and a readiness to share material possessions on the basis of need (Acts 4:32 ff.). Sharing of goods in the early church has been called a "communistic experiment." If communism in the modern sense of the term is meant, nothing could be farther from the truth. For sharing in the common life of the early Christians was the direct result of the baptism of the Spirit, the source and bond of fellowship (Eph. 4:3). There was no compulsory division of property on communistic political principles. It sprang spontaneously out of brotherly love inspired by the Spirit.[15] Moreover there was no wholesale collectivization of goods. As W. O. Carver correctly observes, sales of real estate and personal property were made "from time to time and the distribution was made on the basis of need as the need developed." [16] Hence, all property was held in trust by individual owners until a specific need arose. Finally, the whole "experiment" was soon abandoned by the church because the spirit of the common life began to wane. The "common fund" became a "poor fund," as the accepted practice of the expanding church.

Inequalities on the basis of sex status are abolished by the Spirit. At Pentecost the Spirit came upon men and women alike, fulfilling the prophecy of Joel (Acts 2:17–18). And Paul declared that there is "neither male nor female; for you are all one in Christ Jesus" (Gal. 3:28). By the Spirit we all become sons and heirs of the Father (Gal. 4:6–7).

Racial differences are wholly disregarded by the Spirit. At Pentecost he came upon all Jews "from every nation under heaven" (Acts 2:5). Ever since Pentecost the Spirit has been breaking down racial prejudices and barriers. Though it was "unlawful for a Jew to associate with or visit any one of another nation," Peter visited the Gentile Cornelius, and baptized him and his friends. Peter later explained the whole incident by saying, "Truly I perceive that God shows no partiality, but in every nation any one who fears him and does what is right is acceptable to him" (Acts 10:34). He further defended his action by asserting, "And the Spirit told me to go with them without hesitation [discrimination]" (Acts 11:12). He then concluded, "If then God gave the same gift to them as he gave to us when we believed in the Lord Jesus Christ, who was I that I could withstand God?" (Acts 11:17). Hence, it is not race but rather the action of the Spirit and faith which determine participation in the fellowship of the church.

It is Paul, a Jew, who states the basic principles by which a man is justified: "Or is God the God of the Jews only? Is he not the God of Gentiles also? Yes, of Gentiles also, since God is one; and he will justify the circumcised on the ground of their faith and the uncircumcised because of their faith" (Rom. 3:29–30). For, as Paul says elsewhere, it is by "one Spirit we were all baptized into one body—Jews or Greeks, slaves or free—and all were made to drink of one Spirit" (1 Cor. 12:13). In this fellowship "there cannot be Greek and Jew . . . barbarian, Scythian, slave, free man, but Christ is all, and in all" (Col. 3:11).

Moreover, the crucified Christ has "broken down the dividing wall of hostility" between the races and is now building a new humanity, a new commonwealth of all races with equality of citizenship.[17]

What has been said about the Holy Spirit and race in the early church applies equally to national divisions. Israel was intensely nationalistic, notwithstanding the fact that the prophets taught that God is active in the destiny of other nations (Amos 9:7; Isa. 19:24 f.).[18] Following the emphasis of the prophets, Jesus envisioned all nations under the sovereignty of God. Joseph Klausner, the Jewish scholar, complains that Jesus annulled "both *Judaism* as a *life-force* of the Jewish nation, and also the nation itself as a nation." [19] He concludes that this nonnational character of Jesus' teaching was why the Jews rejected him.[20] When Jesus declared that "God is Spirit," the three particularisms of all religions were, as C. J. Wright states, "transcended, the particularisms of *place, race,* and *book*." [21] To these should be added the particularism of rabid nationalism. For while Jesus expressed patriotic attitudes (Matt. 23:37; Luke 13:34), his patriotism was free from "all particularism and national fanaticism." [22]

The Holy Spirit and Contemporary Ethics

The early church was Spirit-centered. Its ethic was an ethic of the Holy Spirit. As time passed, the Spirit became peripheral and secondary in the life of the church. Toward the end of the first century, the Logos doctrine tended to supplant the Spirit as the life force of the churches. By the time of the Middle Ages the Logos had become a metaphysical principle rather than a living personal Lord whose work was made effective by the Spirit. Today, organized effort, rather than the power of the Spirit, has tended to become the pattern of the church. The Spirit has been retained as a doctrine without being effective in Christian experience.

Consequently, the role of the Spirit has become peripheral in the Christian's moral life. Recovery of the Spirit as the central moral force in the church and the individual is imperative. This would place Christian ethics in its true perspective. Only then will Christian ethics recover its radical theocentricity. For every ethical consideration has its connection with "the whole Idea of God." [23] Only then does God, Son, and Holy Spirit become the ultimate ground of Christian action.

The Holy Spirit alone can provide an adequate dynamic for the Christian's ethical life. Without the energizing work of the Spirit, ethics remains abstract and ineffective. With the Spirit, it is possible to follow out the ethical intentions of Jesus. Once the early Christians responded to the new morality of the Spirit, they rose above the conventional social standards of their day.

Again, the Spirit saves ethics from both legalism and antinomianism. Brunner has rightly observed: "As the Scripture without the Spirit produces false legalism . . . so the Spirit without the Scriptures produces false Antinomianism, and fanaticism." [24] The Spirit's work is always consistent with and constitutes "an extension of the work of Jesus." [25] The Spirit, therefore, does not function contrary to Jesus as Lord, but in harmony with him and his moral teaching.

Any notion that the Spirit leads to either legalism or antinomianism may be dispelled by a careful study of the Gospel of John. Jesus promises that when "the Spirit of truth comes, he will guide into all truth" (John 16:13); that is to say, "not into further new truth, but into the whole truth concerning that which was correctly and concisely set forth by the Son of God." [26] And the statement that the Spirit will declare "the things that are to come" (John 16:13b) probably includes moral truth and guidance where specific biblical teaching is not explicit.[27] For the Paraclete will take the truth of Christ and disclose it to the disciples (John 16:15). To be guided by the Spirit, therefore, is to be led into a knowledge of the will of God as revealed in Christ.

Finally, through the action of the Spirit, Christ becomes our Eternal Contemporary to aid us in moral decisions. Karl Heim has rightly asserted that the Holy Spirit is "the encompassing medium or continuum in which we can have direct contact with Jesus, and it is only in that moment-to-moment contact with our Leader that we can have any knowledge of God at all." [28] Paul states the source of the knowledge of the will of God as follows:

. . . no one comprehends the thoughts of God except the Spirit of God. Now we have received . . . the Spirit which is from God, that we might understand the gifts bestowed on us by God. And we impart this in words not taught by human wisdom but taught by the Spirit, interpreting spiritual truths to those who possess the Spirit (1 Cor. 2:11–13).

Only through the continuing Spirit of Christ can we discover the will of God for us in solving the moral issues of our time.

References

1. F. R. Barry, *The Relevance of Christianity; An Approach to Christian Ethics* (London: Nisbet & Co., Ltd., 1931), p. 102.

2. T. W. Manson, *The Teaching of Jesus; Studies of Its Form and Content* (Cambridge: University Press, 1935), p. 305.

3. E. F. Scott, *The Spirit in the New Testament* (London: Hodder & Stoughton, 1923), p. 26.

4. See H. Wheeler Robinson, *The Christian Experience of the Holy Spirit* (New York: Harper & Bros., 1928), p. 5 ff.

5. Norman H. Snaith, *et. al.,* "The Spirit of God in Jewish Thought," *The Doctrine of the Holy Spirit* (London: Epworth Press, 1941), p. 16.

6. H. B. Swete, *The Holy Spirit in the New Testament* (London: Macmillan Co., 1910), p. 292.

7. A. M. Hunter, *Paul and His Predecessors* (London: Nicholson & Watson, 1940), p. 112.

8. A. M. Hunter, *Interpreting Paul's Gospel* (Philadelphia: Westminster Press, 1954), p. 40.

9. Swete, *op. cit.,* p. 341; See also Galatians 6:18; Philippians 2:1–5; 2 Timothy 4:22.

10. Lindsay Dewar, *An Outline of New Testament Ethics* (Philadelphia: Westminster Press, 1949), p. 101.

11. Scott, *op. cit.,* p. 142.

12. *Ibid.,* p. 164.

13. Floyd Filson, *The New Testament Against Its Environment* (London: S.C.M. Press, 1950), p. 96. Note that after Pentecost Christians never again resorted to lot-casting as an aid in making decisions.

14. Scott, *op. cit.,* p. 164.

15. R. B. Rackham, *The Acts of the Apostles* (12th ed.; London: Methuen & Co., 1935), pp. 41–42.

16. W. O. Carver, *The Acts of the Apostles* (Nashville: Sunday School Board, 1916), p. 35.

17. W. O. Carver, *The Glory of God in the Christian Calling* (Nashville: Broadman Press, 1949), p. 116.

18. A universal fellowship of nations is conceived in Isaiah 40–66; See W. A. L. Elmslie, "Ethics," *Record and Revelation,* ed. H. Wheeler Robinson (London: Oxford Press, 1951), p. 300 f.

19. Joseph Klausner, *Jesus of Nazareth* (New York: Macmillan Co., 1946), p. 390.

20. *Ibid.*

21. "The Gospel According to St. John: Text and Commentary," *The Mission and Message of Jesus,* ed. H. D. A. Major, *et. al.* (New York: E. P. Dutton & Co., Inc., 1938), p. 748.

22. L. H. Marshall, *The Challenge of New Testament Ethics* (New York: Macmillan Co., 1947), p. 158 f.

23. Emil Brunner, *The Divine Imperative* (Philadelphia: Westminster Press, 1947), p. 85.

24. *Ibid.,* p. 92.

25. Filson, *op. cit.,* p. 74; cf. 1 Corinthians 12:3.

26. Edwyn C. Hoskyns, *The Fourth Gospel* (London: Faber & Faber, Ltd., 1947), p. 485.

27. See R. H. Strachan, *The Fourth Gospel* (London: S.C.M. Press, Ltd., 1941), p. 295.

28. Cited by D. M. Baillie, *God Was In Christ* (New York: Charles Scribner's Sons, 1948), p. 99.

Recommended Reading

BARTH, KARL, *The Holy Ghost and the Christian Life.* Translated by R. B. HOYLE. London: Saunders, 1938.

CONNER, W. T., *The Work of the Holy Spirit.* Nashville: Broadman Press, 1949.

DILLISTONE, F. W., *The Holy Spirit in the Life of Today.* Philadelphia: Westminster Press, 1947.

Fison, J. E., *The Blessing of the Holy Spirit.* New York: Longmans, Green & Co., 1950.

Scott, E. F., *The Spirit in the New Testament.* London: Hodder & Stoughton, 1923.

Swete, H. B., *The Holy Spirit in the New Testament.* London: Macmillan Co., 1919.

Part Two: Problems

XI

Duties to Self

Two facts should now be clear about the nature of the Christian ethic: its principle is the will of God as love and its power the Holy Spirit. Love is the basic ethical principle and the Spirit is the enabling power of Christian living. Ethical principles, therefore, must be related to moral action through the dynamic of the Spirit. Jesus' view of a hypocrite, according to C. A. A. Scott, is one who refuses "the guidance of the Holy Spirit in the application of the principle of love to duty." [1] This and subsequent chapters will be devoted to the relation of Christian principles to the problems of contemporary existence.

Duty to self is a crucial issue in Christian ethics. Basic to the problem is the meaning of self-love and selfless love. Which of these types of love is central in Christian ethics? Does selfless love rule out duties to self? An attempt is made in this chapter to give practical answers to these questions.

Self-love Versus Selfless Love

Concerning the fundamental nature of biblical love, scholars are divided into two major camps. On the one hand there are those who maintain that Christian love is purely selfless, allowing no place for considerations of self. It is reasoned that, since God loves us who are unworthy beings, his love is unmotivated, uncalculating, and wholly unselfish. Thus, love is solely an outgoing neighbor-love. On the other hand, there are men who argue that self-love is clearly taught in the Scriptures. It is contended that this love has a craving spirit or the desire for some sort of good. Without this element of desire, it is argued, there can be no duties to self and, thus, no moral sense in the term love.

The Self-love Theory

Exponents of the self-love idea appeal to both the Old and New Testaments. A favorite text is cited from Leviticus 19:18: "You shall love your neighbor as yourself." In the New Testament, it is noted that Jesus sums up the law and the prophets in terms of love to God and love to neighbor as one loves himself (Matt. 22:37–40). Paul likewise compresses all the commandments into one sentence: "You shall love your neighbor as yourself" (Rom. 13:9).

Augustine [2] claims that in the "great" and the "second" injunctions (Matt. 22:37–40; Mark 12:28–33; Luke 10:25–37) there are actually three commands: love to God, to neighbor, and to self. Both love of self and of others is based upon the presence of God in the human heart. Self-love, then, means loving God in ourselves, and the love of others means loving God in them.

Professor A. C. Knudson agrees in principle with Augustine's notion of love, viewing the disjunction of agape and Eros as a false abstraction. He thinks that the divine sanctity of the soul imposes the obligation of love of self and applies to others as well.[3] Moreover, he asserts that Christian love, completely detached from the idea of worth, and duties to self have no moral or rational basis. He concludes that Christian love presupposes an ethical ideal which each one must seek to realize for himself: namely, self-realization through self-sacrifice.[4]

The late L. H. Marshall also makes a place for self-love, contending that Jesus is not so unreasonable as to demand its complete elimination. Rather he demands complete subordination of self-love to love of God and man. It is undue self-love, maintains Marshall, that Jesus condemns. Such inordinate egoism is, he concludes, the root of all evil.[5]

The Theory of Selfless Love

Among the advocates of selfless love are Martin Luther, Leo Tolstoy, and Anders Nygren. Luther's basic concern is to make a clear distinction between the Roman Catholic theory of acquisitive self-love (a synthesis of agape and Eros) and theocentric, self-giving love. He concludes that self-love is not a natural ordinance of God in nature, but a devilish perversion.[6] Tolstoy advocates unclaiming, non-resisting, non-preferential love of neighbor. He defines Christian love as a preference for others over one's self, concluding that genuine love is a present activity only. Hence, future love does not exist.[7] Self-love, in Nygren's opinion, is man's natural condition as well as the basis of the perversion of his will to evil. Hence, in the command to "love thy neighbor as thyself" love is turned from self to neighbor and thus the natural perversity of the will is overcome. Neighborly love, therefore, instead of including self-love, actually excludes and overcomes it.[8]

The New Commandment and Agape-love

There are apparent problems in both doctrines of self-love and selfless love. The former tends to boil down to a prudential ethic. The measure of love for self becomes the standard of love for others. Since most people naturally "look out for self," this is a precarious criterion of conduct. Too, it is difficult to give a satisfactory answer as to how one is to love himself properly.

The selfless love theory tends to belittle the self, denying the validity of self-acceptance and self-realization. Modern psychiatrists and psychologists have been quick to point out this fact. Self-rejection, they claim, is morbid, repressive to one's confidence and efficiency, making one less valuable to the service of God and neighbor. Eric Fromm, for example, insists that if it is a virtue to love one's neighbor as a human being, it must be a virtue "to love myself, since I am a human being too." [9] In support of Fromm, Paul Johnson, a Christian psychologist, observes, that the "Second Commandment" does not read "Love thy neighbor *instead* of thyself, but As you love yourself, love *also* your neighbor." [10]

Psychiatrists and psychologists, however, deny selfless love because they tend to approach the problem from the human side. From the divine perspective the theologian sees a distinct type of love, a love not wholly unrelated to duties to self. This unique type of love is epitomized by our Lord in John 13:34: "A new commandment I give to you, that you love one another; even as I have loved you." The differentia of the Christian ethic is that of love to one another, *not as we love ourselves* but *as Christ loves us*. Such love transcends self-love in the same manner as it transcends the law. H. Richard Niebuhr rightly declares that the author of the Fourth Gospel, discerning that the Jewish statement "Love thy neighbor as thyself" fitted adequately neither Jesus' actions nor his requirements, changed the commandment to read, "Love one another as I have loved you." [11] Thus, the new ethic of Christ "altered the whole moral landscape." [12]

A closer analysis of the "new commandment" reveals its significance as the ground of Christian action. It is new (*kainēn*) in meaning as to form and substance.[13] It is new in that it is given within the context of the new covenant just prior to the Lord's supper. It is new in its measure of love for others, "as I have loved you." Thus the measure of love for others is the love of Christ for us. The *quality* and *direction* of God's love in Christ is revealed in John 3:16 and is to be reproduced in human action.[14] Martin Luther puts it: ". . . each should become a Christ to the other, that we may be Christs to one another and Christ may be the same to all; that is that we may be truly Christian." [15] The commandment is new in that Jesus gives love a surer basis than it has in the Jewish commandment to love one's neighbor as one does himself. Christ himself becomes the basis of love for neighbor.

It is argued that to love "one another" (*allalous*), as the text states, applies only to love among Christians, and therefore, is preferential and particularistic love. Paul Ramsey, for instance, says that this love suffers from "in group" limitations, while the Synoptics and Paul portray a more universal love.[16] But it must be noted that the "new commandment" is in perfect harmony with Jesus' universal and unqualified demand to love neighbor and enemy (Matt. 5:43–48). As F. D. Maurice notes, the commandment requires "greater force and grandeur [than Old Testament love] . . . grounded on that revelation of Christ the Head and

Brother of all men." [17] Therefore, as E. C. Hoskyns declares, the commandment is "no retrograde and narrow exclusivism," but involves all mankind.[18]

It is also argued that Paul accepts the Jewish principle of love of neighbor as oneself. He does say that all commandments are summed up in one sentence: "You shall love your neighbor as yourself" (Rom. 13:9). This negative concept of love, however, is not Paul's own, but Jewish. He is simply appropriating this Jewish command to show that where the basic Christian demand of love has become a reality, there the innermost nature of the law has been fully satisfied and fulfilled. In this sense, Paul shows that the basic demands of the law are also binding upon Christians. For one who loves does no evil to his neighbor; thus "love is fulfilling of the law" (Rom. 13:10; note that there is no article before "law" in the Greek). The same view is found in Matthew 7:12 and Luke 6:31 which gives a positive statement of Hillel's negative "Golden Rule." [19]

Are we left, then, with a love which rules out all consideration of self? Hardly, for agape-love is not wholly unrelated to responsibility for the state of one's own welfare. Confusion arises at the point of identifying agape-love, when directed toward self, with self-depression or self-annihilation. To the contrary, agape-love unifies the divided self and brings it to true self-realization. Yielding the self to God does not mean its destruction, for the "I" is still the one for whom Christ died. And when God accepts man, it makes possible true self-acceptance and self-respect. As in the case of the prodigal son who "came to himself," the divided self is recovered and restored. For God does not give his sons "a spirit of timidity but a spirit of power and love and self-control" (2 Tim. 1:7).

Moreover, self-denial in the theological sense is not self-destruction but true self-realization. By putting the kingdom of God first, the old self transcends itself in devotion to God and neighbor. Thus, self-denial has nothing to do with the achievement of holiness in terms of withdrawal from life or the destruction of self. Rather, it is radical turning away from egoism to theocentrism in which God thrusts the believer in the direction of neighbor and community where the self finds fulfilment in service.

Confusion arises again when agape-love is identified with selfish love, as the former is directed toward self. Concern and care for oneself in the sense of agape-love is not selfishness, since the motive for such is in order to be of service to God and neighbor. To care responsibly for oneself in this sense cannot possibly be construed as being selfish or sinful. Jesus himself urged his disciples to rest from the most sublime service (Mark 6:31). And Paul admonished the young minister to "take heed" to himself in order to make certain that he is growing in the grace of personal character and teaching, so as to save both himself and his hearers (1 Tim. 4:16). To be at one's highest and best self for God requires responsible care and constructive cultivation of one's own personality. Such care of self is not contradictory to agape-love as the central motivation of life.

Some Specific Duties to Self

Agape-love requires that one properly care for himself so as to achieve the highest possible development of one's potentialities for the sake of service to God and man. Such concern and care of self turns out to be more of a duty to God than to self.

The Body

It follows, then, that the Christian has the obligation to God to care properly for his own body. Paul declares that the believer's body belongs to God (1 Cor. 6:13), that it is the temple of the Holy Spirit (1 Cor. 6:19), and that it is to be offered in service to God as "a living sacrifice" (Rom. 12:1). It is imperative, therefore, that the believer strive to present a strong body to God for his glory and service.

Suicide is a violation of the Christian ethic of love as well as the sixth commandment. A man's life is not his own to do with as he wishes. Rather it is a trust from God for which he must give an account. Too, his life is related to other lives. His passing affects the lives of others, especially those of his immediate family. No man lives to himself nor does he die to himself. Moreover, suicide frustrates the purpose of God through the individual. It also shows a lack of trust in the providence of God and is a failure to demonstrate patience to wait for the end of life.

Involved in the proper care of self is the right of self-protection. Emil Brunner takes the position that the Christian has no right of self-defense. However, one may act in self-defense, not as a Christian, but as a citizen for the sake of justice within society. When the latter is not the point at issue, the Christian must simply endure wrong.[20] Thus, only as a representative of the state may one "resist evil." But this position results in an untenable moral dualism. In the light of agape-love, which never circumvents justice, it is the duty of the Christian to defend himself at the personal as well as the civil level where justice is at stake.

At least a preferential ethic of protection and resistance is nascent in the teaching of Jesus. He certainly used some sort of compulsion when he drove the traders out of the Temple (Matt. 21:12–13; Mark 11:15–19; Luke 19:45; John 2:13–17). It appears, therefore, that Jesus had a place for the use of physical force motivated by a holy purpose. On at least three occasions he manifested anger: against inhumanity claiming the sanction of religion (Mark 3:5); against those standing in the way of little children seeking to come to him (Mark 10:14); and against those who use religion for oppression and material gain (Mark 11:15). And Jesus stated that, if the good man had known what hour the thief would enter, he would not have permitted his house to be broken up (Matt. 24:43; Luke 12:39). While the central teaching of this small parable is that of alertness and preparedness for the coming day of the Lord, it would not be *eisegesis* to say that Jesus would approve of a man's protecting his own family, since such action would be within the structure of love and justice. Christian love should, at times and in keeping with justice, adopt physical methods of protection and resistance where responsibility for the care of others is concerned.

The Mind

It is the Christian's responsibility to develop his mind and to sharpen his intellect. He has the moral obligation to be intelligent.

Paul admonishes believers not to be "children in understanding
. . . but in understanding be men" (1 Cor. 14:20, KJV). To
love God with the mind implies the responsibility to think accurately and to discipline one's prejudices and emotions. To
achieve this kind of mind involves the reading of serious literature which will stimulate understanding and develop wisdom.

The Devotional Life

The cultivation of one's own spiritual life is a duty to God.
Speaking to believers, Paul says: "Work out your own salvation
with fear and trembling" (Phil. 2:12). That is to say, "Work
out what God has worked in you." Salvation may be "free,"
but the Christian is under obligation to use every effort to labor
for his own perfection. The basis and dynamic for working out
one's salvation is God—not one's own strength. For God works
all the while in the Christian, supplying the energy. "Both to will
and to work for his good pleasure" (Phil. 2:13). The goal of
salvation is the kind of personality which has as its measure the
stature of the fullness of Christ (Eph. 4:13).

Among the practical means of growth toward the standard of
Christ's perfect life are: the reading of the Word of God, personal
and family devotions, active churchmanship, stewardship of
possessions, and personal witnessing in the power of the Spirit.
Some of the classics of devotional literature which will help to
strengthen the spiritual life are: John Bunyan's *Grace Abound-
ing,* Walter Rauschenbusch's *Prayers of the Social Awakening,*
John Oldham's *Devotional Diary,* and John Wesley's *Journal.*

The duties described above are primarily duties to God. To
give a worthy service to God and neighbor, one must develop his
personality to the fullest possible measure. Responsible care of self
for the glory of God is not "selfish love" and is within the sphere
of agape-love in which sphere one's real self is realized.

References

1. C. A. A. Scott, *New Testament Ethics* (Cambridge: University Press, 1936), p. 47.

2. "On Christian Doctrine," *The Nicene and Post-Nicene Fathers*, ed. Philip Schaff (Grand Rapids: Wm. B. Eerdmans Publishing Co., 1956), II, 529.

3. A. C. Knudson, *The Principles of Christian Ethics* (New York: Abingdon Press, 1943), p. 178.

4. *Ibid.*, p. 132.

5. L. H. Marshall, *The Challenge of New Testament Ethics* (New York: Macmillan Co., 1947), pp. 32–33.

6. *D. Martin Luther's Werke* (Weimar, Germany: Hermann Böhlou, 1892), V, 38, lines 13–15.

7. L. N. Tolstoi, *On Life, and Essays on Religion* (World's Classics), trans. Aylmer Maude (Oxford: University Press, 1934), pp. 97–98; 102–103.

8. A. T. S. Nygren, *Agape and Eros,* trans. Philip S. Watson (Philadelphia: Westminster Press, 1953), p. 101.

9. Erich Fromm, *The Art of Loving* (New York: Harper & Bros., 1956), p. 58.

10. P. E. Johnson, *Christian Love* (New York: Abingdon Press, 1951), p. 39.

11. H. R. Niebuhr, *Christ and Culture* (New York: Harper & Bros., 1951), p. 18.

12. A. J. Gossip, "The Gospel According to St. John," *Interpreters Bible* (New York: Abingdon Press, 1952), VIII, 693.

13. J. H. Thayer, *A Greek-English Lexicon of the New Testament* (New York: Harper & Bros., 1886), p. 317.

14. C. H. Dodd, *The Gospel and the Law* (New York: Columbia University Press, 1950), p. 71.

15. "Treatise on Christian Liberty," *Works of Martin Luther* (Philadelphia: A. J. Holman, 1916), p. 338.

16. Paul Ramsey, *Basic Christian Ethics* (New York: Charles Scribner's Sons, 1950), p. 20.

17. F. D. Maurice, *The Epistles of St. John* (London: Macmillan Co., 1867), pp. 98–99.

18. Edwyn C. Hoskyns, *The Fourth Gospel,* ed. F. N. Davey (London: Faber & Faber, 1947), II, 530.

19. *Tobit* 4:15.

20. Emil Brunner, *The Divine Imperative* (Philadelphia: Westminster Press, 1947), p. 691.

Recommended Reading

HARKNESS, GEORGIA, *Christian Ethics*. New York: Abingdon Press, 1957, Chapter 6.

KIERKEGAARD, SOREN, *Works of Love*. Translated by DAVID F. SWENSON and LILLIAN SWENSON. Princeton: Princeton University Press, 1946.

KNUDSON, A. C., *The Principles of Christian Ethics*. New York: Abingdon Press, 1943, Chapter 9.

NYGREN, ANDRES, *Agape and Eros*. Translated by PHILIP S. WATSON. Philadelphia: Westminster Press, 1953.

XII

Marriage and the Family

The family is the most intimate and significant of all human relations. It is the cell unit of society and the matrix of personality. No one can develop into a person outside the fellowship of other persons. Thus God "setteth the solitary in families" (Psalm 68:6, KJV). This chapter is concerned with the Christian conception of marriage and family relationships, including divorce, sex, and tensions arising in family living.

The Biblical Basis of Marriage

Marriage is a divinely ordained relationship or union (Gen. 1:27–28; 2:18–24). Created man needed a counterpart, a "helpmeet," or a "helper fit for him." God made woman from man and "brought her unto him." Marriage, therefore, is God-given. Of woman Adam declared, "This at last is bone of my bones, and flesh of my flesh," signifying essential unity and responsibility. "Therefore," adds the inspired writer, man "leaves his father and his mother and cleaves to his wife, and they become one flesh" (Gen. 2:24). D. S. Bailey calls this "one flesh" relationship the mysterious *henosis* (union, becoming one) the ontological basis of marriage.[1] In this unique union, man and woman become one, yet do not lose their individuality. In marriage, one finds oneself in another so that each becomes the *alter ego* of the other.

The Purpose of Marriage

The ends of marriage are already set forth in the Scriptures. The primary object of marriage, according to the earliest creation

111

narrative (Gen. 2:18,22), is that of companionship. God provides an intimate, personal relation between husband and wife for their mutual enrichment and fulfilment. Another purpose of marriage is that of procreation and rearing of children. The injunction, "Be fruitful and multiply, and fill the earth" (Gen. 1:28), was taken seriously by the Jews who were concerned for the preservation of the family. Constructive sexual fulfilment is a third purpose of marriage. The intensity of the sex drive in man is greater than is necessary to carry on the race. Marriage provides a continuous form of association for man and woman in which the powerful sex urge is sublimated so that it may serve to meet human needs and to avoid disrupting personality and society.

Some of the church fathers—Augustine, for example—tended to restrict the sexual act to procreation; but later it was held allowable for the satisfaction of lust which proceeds from incontinence. Thus marriage guarded husband and wife from adultery and fornication. A basic purpose of marriage, therefore, was conceived to be a "remedy against sin."

The Foundations of Marriage

Christian marriage rests upon four fundamental principles. It is grounded in the principle of monogamy, the binding together of one man and one woman in the marital relationship. Monogamous marriage is the standard set by Jesus and the early church (Matt. 19:4–6; 1 Cor. 7:10). Today this pattern of marriage is being challenged by "free-lovers" who talk about the "monotony of monogamy," claiming that "extra-marital" relationships may be not only lawful but healthful. But convincing arguments for the monogamic pattern are obvious. It is grounded in creation (Matt. 19:4 ff.); every child needs *his* father and *his* mother for the full development of personality; human sexual love is in essence monistic;[2] and the stability of the family and nation depends upon the kind of union which monogamy provides.

There is the principle of permanency in Christian marriage. In the New Testament, marriage is conceived as the binding together of one man and one woman on a permanent basis. It is a lifelong commitment which death alone terminates. More will be said about this basis of marriage in the later discussion about divorce.

Fidelity is another ground of Christian marriage. Emil Brunner holds that fidelity is the fundamental basis of every true marriage. When based solely on love, marriage is lost from the outset. However, no marriage, he thinks, should be consummated without both fidelity and love.[3] Faithfulness in thought, as well as action, on the part of both husband and wife is the Christian demand. Jesus condemns not only the adulterous act, but also the "lustful look" (Matt. 5:27 f.).

The ultimate ground of marriage is that of love (agape-love). This kind of love is more than mere affection or an emotional impulse. It is love which expresses itself by an attitude of considerateness, trust, mutual helpfulness, justice, and forgiveness. It is the motive which inspires concern for the spiritual, as well as the physical, life (Eph. 5:21–33); it is also the principle for the discipline and spiritual growth of offspring, and the obedience of children to parents (Eph. 6:1 f.). In short, love is the supreme motive and controlling spirit of the husband-wife and parent-child relationships (Col. 3:19 f.).

Divorce and Remarriage

One of the knotty problems in the teaching of Jesus is that of divorce. Four brief passages furnish the basic evidence for his attitude toward this issue (Matt. 5:31–32; 19:3–12; Mark 10:2–12; and Luke 16:18). In Mark and Luke, Jesus categorically states that whoever divorces his wife and remarries commits adultery, or commits adultery against his wife. The two passages in Matthew introduce the so-called "exception clause"—"except for unchastity" (RSV), "saving for the cause of fornication" (KJV). The question arises as to whether the "saving clause" in Matthew is valid or an addition. Mark and Luke do not record this exception. Does Matthew contradict or supplement Mark and Luke? To answer adequately this question, it is necessary to probe into the background out of which the question of divorce arises.

In the time of Jesus' ministry, a heated debate about divorce was in progress. Hence, the Pharisees came to Jesus asking, "Is it lawful to divorce one's wife for any cause?" This question had provoked a constant battle between the two great rabbinical schools, the Hillel and the Shammai. It grew out of a difference of interpretation of the law in Deuteronomy 24:1 f. The Hillel (liberal) school took the passage to mean that a husband could divorce his wife for almost any cause. For instance, Rabbi Hillel held that if the wife burned the biscuits or put too much salt in the soup, the husband had grounds for divorce. Rabbi Akiba (died about A.D. 135) allowed a man to divorce his wife if he found a woman more beautiful! The Shammai (conservative) school allowed a man to divorce his wife only if he discovered something unchaste in her life. The important phrase in Deuteronomy was the "unseemly thing" which meant adultery in the thought of the Shammaians.

In his reply to the question on divorce, Jesus took a position high above the whole debate, referring back to God's divine intention and ideal of marriage (Gen. 2:24). Jesus' critics promptly reminded him that Moses "commanded" the writing of a "bill of divorcement." Whereupon Jesus pointed out that Moses "suffered" or allowed divorce as an unwilling concession to human weakness, "for the hardness of your heart." This was actually an amelioration of woman's state, conferring upon her a certain right. If she were simply dismissed, her lot would be hard indeed, for no man would take her into his household. Hence, she was to be given a "separation notice," or certificate stating that she was no longer claimed by her husband, and was therefore under no obligation or tie to him.[4]

Thus, what Jesus did was to set forth God's divine ideal of marriage which is binding upon all believers. "Have you not read," he asked, "that he who made them from the beginning made them male and female, and said, 'For this reason a man shall leave his father and mother and be joined to his wife, and the two shall become one'? So they are no longer two but one. What therefore God has joined together, let no man put asunder" (Matt. 19:4–6; cf. Gen. 2:24).

Against this apparent teaching of the indissolubility of marriage, Matthew makes one exception in the "saving clause." Did

Jesus utter it? Numerous arguments pro and con are presented by the scholars. In support of the authenticity of the Matthean statement, there are the following views: first, it is in the Bible and therefore must be true; second, Matthew got this clause from the lost document Q, the main source of the non-Marcan part of Matthew's gospel and the original material of Mark; third, "fornication" in the clause is not adultery, but refers to the unfaithfulness on the part of the woman prior to marriage and, when discovered subsequently, the husband is required to put her away because in God's sight there has been no true marriage. She is allegedly married to the first man with whom she had sexual intercourse, and to "marry" during the lifetime of the man is to commit adultery. "Causeth her to commit adultery" means to make her to be an adultress and the man who divorces such a wife proclaims to the world that she belonged to another before "marrying" him; fourth, it is the one and only rule which Jesus laid down and, therefore, the one exception to the rule that he did not lay down laws but guiding principles; fifth, it is a valid clause in which Jesus sanctions separation but not divorce as in the teaching of the Roman Church; sixth, whether the "saving clause" is original or not, it is probably true to Jesus' thought.

Exponents who deny the originality of the exception clause declare that it is an interpolation or addition from Matthew himself. These hypotheses are supported for several reasons: (1) Matthew, writing to the Jews, tones down the absolute teaching on divorce to bring it more into agreement with their customs, or to make it harmonize with the conservative view of the Shammai school; (2) Mark, the oldest Gospel, and Luke do not contain the clause; (3) Paul, the apostle, knows nothing of this clause and supports Mark and Luke against Matthew (1 Cor. 7:10 f.), actually referring to the Lord's teaching (cf. Rom. 7:2–3); (4) it is inconceivable that Mark and Luke would have omitted from their writings such an important exception, had Jesus actually taught it; (5) it is easier to suppose that there has been an interpolation in Matthew than to suppose that it is suppressed or overlooked by Mark and Luke; (6) the surprise of the disciples (Matt. 19:10) is difficult to explain if Jesus had merely reaffirmed the conservative view of the Shammai school with which they were acquainted. The amazement would have been natural if the statement on divorce had been made absolute for the first time; (7) it is legalistic and therefore opposed to the whole context in which Jesus is laying down great principles, not laws; and (8) finally, it is out of harmony with Jesus' attitude toward such persons as the woman at the well and the woman taken in adultery (John 4:7–26; 8:3–11).

The weight of evidence appears to be against the validity of the "saving clause" in Matthew. It certainly is in opposition to Jesus' ideal of marriage as that of one man and one woman on a permanent basis. As we have seen, he appealed to the primordial law of monogamic marriage, an indissoluble bond between man and wife so long as they live. Thus God's original will is restored for marital relations.

It must be borne in mind that Jesus was not legislating, but setting forth the ideal of marriage. This ideal is impossible for persons married and divorced before commitment to Christ. And in the case of a very bad marriage, love, not law, must rule. In some instances, it may be the more decent thing to seek a divorce. But no divorce should be sought until an impasse has been reached and all reasonable means have been used to save the marriage.

As for remarriage, Jesus does not make this clear. Contention for remarriage after divorce can only be by an argument from silence and inference. Paul indicates that in the case of separation the parties must remain in that state or be reconciled (1 Cor. 7:10–11). He permits remarriage only in the case of widows, but holds that the new husband must be a Christian (1 Cor. 7:39). The so-called "Pauline privilege" allows for separation when the unbelieving partner chooses it (1 Cor. 7:15). The believer is "not bound." It is argued that this phrase, "is not bound," gives the individual the right to remarry, but this goes against the grain of Paul's total teaching on marriage.

Augustine took the view that all marriages are indissoluble by natural law.[5] This position is held by the Roman Catholic Church to this day. The Eastern Fathers of the church interpreted the

"Pauline privilege" as a complete dissolution, carrying with it, by inference, freedom of remarriage. Protestant churches generally take the position of the Eastern Fathers.

The Christian View of Sex

Social scientists have taught us much about sexuality and love. Yet there is an enormous amount of ignorance about these forces in human life. Strong, divergent views prevail concerning the nature, purpose, and function of sex. Hence, there is an imperative need for an evangelical philosophy of the meaning of sexuality. Professor Otto Piper says that such a philosophy must speak clearly and firmly about the subject itself and be based exclusively on the Bible.[6]

No elaborate sex code can be developed from the teaching of Jesus. But, from the total message of revelation, a general sex ethic emerges. This approach reveals that sex is not an evil, but is good and necessary. Sex is one of God's many gifts to man and a part of man's total personality. Like all instincts, this one is good in itself, for "God looked upon all that he had made and saw that it was good." Sex, however, may become evil if uncontrolled and unregulated by man's higher moral, social, and spiritual purposes. As Professor Roland Bainton states: "Sex is not to be indulged in promiscuously or for private gratification apart from social responsibility. . . . Sex is good but capable of abuse, like every good, and is to be disciplined and subordinated to an entire way of life." [7]

Again, coitus is intended by the Lord as a means of procreation. However, sexual intercourse may also be an expression of the most tender spiritual love between husband and wife. As Elton Trueblood says, "Sexual intercourse . . . provides husband and wife with a *language* which cannot be matched by words or by any other act whatsoever. Love needs language for its adequate expression and sex has its own syntax." [8]

This further word should be said about the Christian meaning of sex. It is the only way in which man shares in God's continuing creative process. The term "procreation" means "creation for and on behalf of" another. Through coitus man functions as God's agent to continue his creative work. This is in accordance with God's command to "replenish and fill the earth."

Celibacy is related to the problem of sex. A brief examination of its biblical and historical role follows. The Old Testament knows nothing of celibacy. Rather, it exalts matrimony. The Lord specifically declares that it is not good for man to be alone (Gen. 2:18). In the New Testament, there is an enigmatic reference to those who have made themselves eunuchs for the kingdom of God (Matt. 19:12). The principle involved appears to be that those who can set aside the desire for marriage to devote their undivided attention for the kingdom of heaven's sake may remain unmarried. If one cannot do this, it would be best for him to marry (cf. 1 Cor. 7:25–28).

Paul is sometimes accused of having an unhealthy attitude toward marriage. But this attitude toward marriage is conditioned by his eschatology and sense of vocation. His expectation of the imminent return of the Lord moved him to urge all to remain in the state or condition they might be when called of God, whether slave or free, whether married or unmarried. Paul's personal preference for the single life was due to his desire to be free to dedicate himself wholly to God's service. But this kind of life, he reminds us, is a "special gift from God, one of one kind and one of another" (1 Cor. 7:7).

In spite of the fact that the Bible teaches that marriage is "honorable" (Heb. 13:4), it has been depreciated in some religious groups; and celibacy has been set up as a central virtue. This tendency to disparage marriage is due to the fact that Greek and Oriental concepts of marriage as evil penetrated into the early church. It was reasoned that, since sex involves the flesh, the sexual act is evil. Thus, in a world of licentiousness, virginity seemed to be the supreme expression of moral power. At the Council of Nicaea, A.D. 325, an attempt was made to compel married bishops to abandon their wives, but it failed. Gregory VII (Hildebrand), Pope from A.D. 1073 to 1085, insisted upon the disposition of all married priests. After his death, the celibacy of both priests and deacons was enjoined by Canon Law. In view of this Roman Catholic demand for celibacy, it is interesting to note that Peter, the apostle most prized by this communion, was married (Matt. 8:14; Luke 4:38; 1 Cor. 9:5).

Celibacy triumphed in the Roman Church, but not without dire results. On the one hand, celibacy resulted in corruption among the clergy. In many places, clerical marriage was simply succeeded by clerical concubinage. In the age of the Renaissance, popes made no secret of concubines and illegitimate children. On the other hand, there was an intensification of the disparagement of the marriage relationship not only among the clergy, but also among the laity in general.[9]

Preparation for Marriage

Preparation for marriage and family living has been sadly neglected in our country. Instead, more attention has been given by writers on the family to marriage problems, particularly to divorce. No doubt, more attention to the preparation of young people for the unique experience of holy matrimony would make for more successful marriages and the reduction of the divorce rate. Research in the field of the family indicates certain guiding principles to successful marriage.

Achievement of Some Degree of Maturity

Emotional immaturity is one of the most troublesome factors in marriage. Obviously, absolute emotional maturity is achieved by no one. However, there are criteria of emotional behavior which tend to be necessary for happiness in marriage. Judson and Mary Landis, sociologists, have spelled out these principles. The mature person, according to their research, is able to be objective; is emotionally independent of parents; makes decisions for himself; acknowledges and takes responsibility for his mistakes; is heterosexual in his sex interests; accepts his chronological age; is willing to wait for future pleasures; profits by his mistakes; accepts the moral codes; tries to understand others; gets along with other people; accepts the present and looks to the future; sees sex expression as a normal and satisfying phase of life; is willing to use reason rather than fantasy in mate selection; and can constructively evaluate himself and his motives.[10]

There should be added to the above list of criteria a word about spiritual maturity. By this is meant a decisive Christian experience. It involves growing in grace and the knowledge of Christ. It also includes active participation in a church and the extension of the gospel of the kingdom of God on earth. Such a growing religious experience is essential on the part of both husband and wife if they are to realize fully the purpose of their marital partnership.

Criteria for the Choice of a Mate

The sage rightly declares that "He who finds a wife finds a good thing . . ." (Prov. 18:22). But how does one go about finding an adequate life mate? The following decalogue of guiding principles for the wise choice of a mate may be helpful: mutual physical attraction; intellectual and cultural affinity; a common religious faith; a fair degree of economic security; a common vocational interest; emotional maturity; wholesome attitudes toward sex and a desire for children; relatively good health; long time contact with wholesome family life; and a relatively long acquaintance and engagement.

There is no finality to the above principles in choosing a mate and one does not have to meet all the conditions to be happily married. But if one is guided by them, marriage will not be a "leap in the dark."

Personality Interaction in the Family

The family is "an arena of interacting personalities." [11] It is a primary group of intimate, informal, spontaneous, face-to-face relationships, characterized by both co-operation and clash of personalities. Wishes and needs of children collide with those of father and mother, and vice versa. William Graham Sumner describes the family as an association based on "antagonistic co-operation" in which individual values are sought.[12]

Husband-Wife Relations

Of all human relationships the husband-wife is the most intimate and testing. Two personalities with individual tastes, desires, opinions, and goals are bound to have some tensions. These tensions may center around such "tremendous trifles" as mannerisms, habits, carelessness, or more serious matters as infidelity, religious differences, and economic difficulties. Here we are concerned with the latter and more serious types of problems in the husband-wife relationship.

Some couples have the fallacious notion that if they do not achieve happy sex adjustment immediately after marriage, they were not made for each other. Professor Judson Landis made a study in which he discovered that it takes more time to work out adjustments in sex than in such areas as the economic, social, or religious. Approximately half of the couples studied by Landis agreed that their sex adjustment had been satisfactory from the beginning. The remainder indicated that months, and in some cases years, passed before a satisfactory adjustment was achieved. Only 6.6 per cent never made the adjustment.[13]

Effort to remodel a mate after marriage is another source of tension. During courtship, certain habits and eccentricities may be tolerated with the idea that after marriage the mate will change. Husband or wife may then attempt to bring about desired changes. The result is usually disappointing. Adults do not easily change their ways. Ordinarily they will possess, in some degree, previous faults and failures which tend to be permanent.

One of the chief causes of marital tension stems from the handling of finances. The amount of income is not so important as the way in which the money is to be spent. One partner may be a spendthrift, the other frugal and saving. Perhaps both tend to live beyond the family income. Or the husband may not fairly share the income which actually belongs to the whole family. These are serious sources of tension and conflict.

Religious differences are also sources of trouble. It is always hazardous to marry across strong religious lines. Divorce rates are more frequent in mixed marriages. Studies show that where both parents were Protestant, 6.8 per cent of parents separated. Where both parents were Roman Catholic, 6.4 per cent of parents separated. In the case of mixed marriages, 15.2 per cent represented broken homes. Where parents had no religious profession,

16.7 per cent of the homes were broken. In short, there was in the case of mixed marriages two and one-fourth times as much separation and divorce as in families where there was religious homogeneity.[14]

There are certain "tension relievers" which may be of help when disagreements arise between mates. A sense of humor is essential. Instead of allowing feelings to find outlet in self-pity, sulkiness, or abuse, they can be expressed in humor. It is a good safety valve to let off pent-up emotions and frustrations.

Trifles and nonessentials should be surrendered. While basic convictions may not be given up, it is necessary that both husband and wife compromise on nonessentials. They can learn to develop the capacity to ignore and forget minor irritations. Acceptance of one another's faults and the capacity to live with them must be learned by every couple.

Wise elimination of the sources of friction is another factor in achieving marital harmony. If there is a physical problem, a physician can be consulted. If a personality problem exists, one may try to see himself objectively and seek a solution to his particular personal weakness. This may require professional help in extreme cases.

Solving problems day by day is important. Tensions should never be allowed to pile up. Rather, they should be solved the day they appear.

Engagement in calm discussions of marital issues will help. Talking about problems and "hearing each other out" are constructive ways of dealing with disagreements. When both insist on talking at once, neither is able to understand the other or to look at the issue intelligently.

Participation in a partnership in which plans are formed jointly is helpful in avoiding tension. The selection of household articles, the choice of a school for the children, and the way in which the division of labor in the home is to be done should always be worked out together.

Practice of Christian ethics in the home would result in genuine fellowship and harmony. Love of husbands for their wives as Christ loves the church (Eph. 5:21 ff.), forgiveness as Christ forgives (Eph. 4:32), good housekeeping (Titus 2:4,5), and service rather than selfishness (Matt. 20:26) are good basic principles to follow in the practice of Christian ethics in the home.

Every couple should attempt to work out problems for themselves. But, if no progress can be made, a wise and trusted friend should be consulted. This person may be a pastor, a doctor, or a competent marriage counselor who can see the problem more objectively and suggest a solution.

Finally, it is important to remember that in every fruitful marriage there will be some tension. Some allowance must be made for it. For marriage is not always a peaceful paradise, but a dynamic adventure.

Parent-Child Relations

Principles for parent-child relations are pointed up by Paul in Ephesians 6:1–4: "Children, obey your parents in the Lord, for this is right. Honor your father and mother. . . . Fathers, do not provoke your children to anger, but bring them up in the discipline and instruction of the Lord." Children owe obedience and respect to both parents. But respect and obedience on the part of children is dependent upon the right exercise of authority by parents. It must be a responsible authority in which the child will feel secure in the love of parents.

Threats to the child's sense of security.—Parents often consciously or unconsciously threaten the child's sense of security. Among these threats is that of rejection, the feeling that he does not belong or is an intruder in the family circle. This threat falls heavily upon three groups: the unwanted child, the illegitimate child, and the adopted child who never develops a full sense of belonging to the family.

There is also the threat of replacement of a child by the birth of a brother or sister. The older child should be prepared emotionally for the arrival of a new sibling. After its arrival, the older child should be assured of the continuing love of parents.

There is the threat of favoritism in the family. The story of Joseph and his brethren shows that it is a very old and dangerous threat. To avoid jealousy and friction, children should be made aware of equal love and understanding on the part of parents.

There is the threat to the child's security in the attempt to hide truth behind a cloud of evasion or mystery. For example, when the child inquires about sex, parents often give a vague or deceptive reply. This makes the child curious and anxious. He can always stand reality better than deception and should be told the truth.

The discipline of children.—Paul urges parents to discipline their children. With the widespread disregard of children for parents, property, and the rights of other people, modern thinkers and writers are beginning to look seriously at the place of discipline in the home. There is a negative type of discipline which may be too harsh and can easily discourage the child, making him sullen, morose, and frustrated (Col. 3:21). Unreasonably lashing a child, denying him a meal, shutting him in a dark room, and shaming him are dubious methods of discipline.

Positive discipline becomes a method of guiding the growth of the child in the way of achieving a mature, independent personality. This kind of discipline has three characteristics: it is firm, consistent, and kind. On occasion some degree of corporal punishment may be necessary. "Spare the rod and spoil the child" is a sounder principle than "never strike a child except in self-defense," as advocated by some pseudo-psychologists.

The spiritual growth of children.—Parents have the responsibility of strengthening the spiritual and moral foundations of the home. This is in keeping with Paul's injunction to bring up children in the "instruction of the Lord." Effective ways of doing this are teaching the child to pray, reading the Scriptures in the family circle, the use of Christian hymns in the home, and group worship (Col. 3:16).

Direct religious teaching in the home is essential. Some parents are too lazy to help their children in this way. Others are bewildered by their children's questions concerning the faith.[15] Too many parents depend on the Sunday school as a substitute for religious instruction in the home. But their responsibility to educate their children religiously is a duty which cannot be delegated. Nor can they discharge their duty in this matter by being mere "pedagogic machines for passing on certain verbal statements about God." [16]

The most effective way of interpreting the Christian faith to children is by parental example. Parental influence does more to shape the child's character than any other force. This is attested to in a survey which reveals five influence areas—parents, friends, club leaders, public and Sunday school teachers—parents are the chief source of the child's knowledge of right and wrong, while the Sunday school teacher makes the least impression.[17]

Moreover, there is little measurable connection between the moral preachments of parents and the conduct of their children. However, there is a close relation between the values, mannerisms, attitudes, and behavior of parents and those of their children.

The Church and the Family

The church has the greatest opportunity of any institution to serve the family and to help improve its quality of life. It can appeal to motives which no other institution can. It has resources to do the job in terms of leadership and facilities which no other agency has.

For one thing, the church can teach the Christian view of sex, marriage, and the family. This can be achieved through home and church-centered literature. Recent publications of the major denominations in the United States reveal a beginning in the direction of a constructive emphasis on the home, marriage, and the family.

A church can provide classes for young people contemplating marriage, for parents at the childbearing stage, and the "launching stage" when the children are going out to make homes of their own. Churches may also observe Family Life Week, sponsor Family Life Institutes (denominational headquarters will furnish information), establish a day nursery, a kindergarten, and a family counseling service.

The pastor can emphasize the biblical teaching on marriage and the family in his sermons, establish a premarital counseling service for young people, and provide forums and classes dealing with such problems as courtship, the engagement, the wedding, the honeymoon, and marital adjustments.

These are only a few practical ways in which churches can help to strengthen the spiritual and moral foundations of the family. Every effort should be made to relate the resources of the churches to family needs. For the future of the churches, as well as civilization, will be determined by the quality of life in the home.

References

1. D. S. Bailey, *The Mystery of Love and Marriage* (New York: Harper & Bros., 1952), pp. 3 ff.

2. Emil Brunner, *The Divine Imperative* (Philadelphia: Westminster Press, 1947), pp. 342 ff.

3. *Ibid.,* p. 344.

4. Theodore H. Robinson, *The Gospel of Matthew* (New York: Harper & Bros., 1928), pp. 158–159.

5. "Adulterous Marriages," in *Saint Augustine: Treatises on Marriage and Other Subjects,* ed. R. J. Deferrari (New York: Fathers of the Church, Inc., 1955), Book 2, Chapter 13, p. 18.

6. Otto Piper, *The Christian Interpretation of Sex* (New York: Charles Scribner's Sons, 1941), pp. ix–x.

7. "Christianity and Sex, An Historical Survey," *Pastoral Psychology,* III (September, 1952), 10.

8. Elton and Pauline Trueblood, *The Recovery of Family Life* (New York: Harper & Bros., 1953), p. 54.

9. See H. C. Lea, *History of Sacerdotal Celibacy in the Christian Church* (London: Watts and Co., 1932).

10. J. T. and M. G. Landis, *Building a Successful Marriage* (New York: Prentice-Hall, 1958), p. 114. See also H. A. Overstreet, *The Mature Mind* (London: Gollancy, 1950), Chapter II, "Criteria of Maturity."

11. Willard Waller and Reuben Hill, *The Family* (revised ed.; New York: The Dryden Press, 1951), p. 25.

12. W. G. Sumner, *Folkways* (New York: Ginn Company, 1906), pp. 345–346.

13. "Length of Time Required to Achieve Adjustment in Marriage," *American Sociological Review,* II (December, 1946), 666–667.

14. James A. Pike, *If You Marry Outside Your Faith* (New York: Harper & Bros., 1954), pp. 27–28; see *Social Forces,* XXI, 334 (1943) and *American Sociological Review,* XIV (1949), 401.

15. See Georgia Harkness, "A Theology for Babes," *Christian Century* (July 29, 1936), pp. 1033–1035.

16. Willard L. Sperry, *What You Owe Your Child* (New York: Harper & Bros., 1934), p. 40.

17. Hugh Hartshorne and Mark A. May, *et al.*, "Testing the Knowledge of Right and Wrong," *Religious Education*, XXI (Oct., 1926), 539–554.

Recommended Reading

BAILEY, D. S., *The Mystery of Love and Marriage.* New York: Harper & Bros., 1952.

JAMES, E. O., *Marriage and Society.* London: Hutchinson's University Library, 1952.

LEWIN, S. H., and GILMORE, JOHN, *Sex Without Fear.* New York: Medical Research Press, 1951.

MACE, DAVID R., *Whom God Hath Joined.* Philadelphia: Westminster Press, 1953.

PIKE, JAMES A., *If You Marry Outside of Your Faith.* New York: Harper & Bros., 1954.

TRUEBLOOD, ELTON and P. C. G., *The Recovery of Family Life.* New York: Harper & Bros., 1953.

WALLER, WILLARD, and HILL, REUBEN, *The Family: A Dynamic Interpretation.* Revised by Reuben Hill, New York: The Dryden Press, 1951.

XIII
Race Relations

Racism, the assumption of inherent racial superiority on the part of certain races and the consequent discrimination against others, is a crucial issue confronting Christianity today. Universal in scope, racism now plagues every continent on the globe.[1] Since it is impossible to discuss here the race issue in world perspective, the material is confined to the Negro-white problem of the United States in light of Christian principles.

The American Dilemma

Gunnar Myrdal, noted Swedish sociologist, calls the race problem in the United States "an American dilemma." As he describes it, the dilemma is due to a discrepancy between the ideals which Americans profess and their practice which contradicts these ideals in intergroup relations. For instance, the "American Creed" stands for liberty, equality, justice, and fair opportunity for all citizens; but there are segments of people who do not share equally in these blessings.[2]

Unfortunately, the churches which have contributed to the development of the "American Creed" are themselves caught in the "American dilemma." Professing that all men have equal dignity and worth in the sight of God, they tend to deny these truths in actual human relations. The result is a guilty conscience that causes Christians to avoid facing reality in race relations.[3]

The Negro in the Nation

The Negro minority, which is among certain racial groups in the United States, feels the heavy hand of discrimination. A brief

128

examination of history shows how Negroes got their present status in society. According to John Smith, *The Generall Historie of Virginia,* Negro slaves were brought to America ahead of the arrival of the Pilgrim Fathers. "A Dutch Man-of-Warre" arrived in Jamestown in 1619, "that sold us twenty negars." Over a period of two centuries there were ever increasing shipments of Negroes from Africa who were to labor in the new world. Today they constitute the largest minority group in America, or ten per cent of the total population of 188,321,000.

After the Civil War, provisional governments were established in the South and were generally controlled by "carpet-baggers." Many whites were disfranchised and freed Negroes were granted suffrage. As a result, Negroes were elected to public office in several states. But, with the General Amnesty Act of 1872, southern whites regained the machinery of the government and succeeded in putting the Negroes back in a place of subordination. They were disfranchised, segregated, and discriminated against in education, economics, politics, health, housing, recreation, and social life.

By the turn of the twentieth century, the pattern of segregation was firmly established. The "separate but equal" ruling of the Supreme Court in the Plessy *versus* Ferguson case of 1896, which decreed that segregation on trains was constitutional so long as equal facilities were provided for Negroes, was applied to all public schools and other public facilities. Thus the stage was set for half a century of almost complete segregation of the Negro in the South.

Recent Court Rulings

On May 17, 1954, the Supreme Court ruled that in the field of public education the "separate but equal" doctrine was unconstitutional. A little more than a year later, May 31, 1955, the Court ruled that the "courts will require that defendants make a prompt and reasonable start toward full compliance with the May 17, 1954 ruling." On November 7, 1955, the Court applied to public parks, beaches, and golf courses the ruling enunciated in the first decision in the school desegregation cases.

This revolutionary action of the Supreme Court revived old movements and stimulated the rise of new ones for and against desegregation. Since the 1954 decision, at least twenty pro-segregation groups have appeared in southern states.[4] The old Ku Klux Klan continues to exist and is attempting to exploit reaction to the Supreme Court's decision. But it is now ineptly led, unmasked by state laws, and closely watched by the Federal Bureau of Investigation. This movement has thus been relegated to the status of a "fringe" group. A new movement known as the White Citizen's Council is far more articulate, active, and effective in its efforts to circumvent the Court's decree. Organized in Indianola, Mississippi in October 1954, the W.C.C. now claims more than 60,000 members. Its stated purpose is "Dedication to the maintenance of peace, good order, and domestic tranquility in our communities and in our state and to the preservation of our state's rights." [5] Its methods in dealing with Negroes include economic pressure while using social and political pressure in dealing with whites. "Economic lynchings" now take the place of physical lynchings of the past years.

The White Citizen's Council's propaganda follows the line that integration of the races will mean the collapse of society. The National Association for the Advancement of Colored People is regarded as an agent of a plot to destroy the white race. The Supreme Court is the "political tool" of the conspirators, while the schools and churches are honeycombed by "neo-communist, neo-socialist teachers and preachers" who aid and abet the movement.

Among the prominent organized movements for racial integration are the National Urban League and the National Association for the Advancement of Colored People. The latter is the most effective agency of the Negro in his struggle for first-class citizenship. Organized in 1909 by some white people, it now boasts of 700 branches, youth councils, and college chapters, with a membership of more than 100,000, largely composed of middle-class Negroes. Through this militant organization, operating within the framework of the democratic ideology, the Negro seeks to eliminate discrimination and segregation in every area of his existence. By 1948, the NAACP had won 23 of 25 major cases before the Supreme Court, but the 1954 decision to desegregate the schools was its greatest victory. In 1958, the organization had an income of over one million dollars to support its staff and program. Its chief periodical, *Crisis,* has been published since 1910.

The Problem of Prejudice

At the root of racism is the fact of prejudice. Derived from the Latin noun, *praejudicium,* meaning judgment based on prior decisions, the term "prejudice" in English took on the idea of prejudgment with the feeling-tone of aversion or hostility. Applied to race, then, prejudice means aversion for an individual or group, predicated upon inadequate knowledge. Usually, a whole group is categorized in terms of a few ideas about one of its members. Such "overcategorization," as Professor Gordon Allport observes, is perhaps the commonest trick of the mind. "Given a thimbleful of facts," he says, "we rush to make generalizations as large as a tub." [6] Thus the prejudiced person makes unwarranted generalizations about a group on the basis of a limited knowledge of an individual member.

The Scope of Prejudice

As for the prevalence of prejudice in the United States, Allport has discovered, on the basis of public opinion poll data, that: ". . . one-fifth of our people are implacable Anglophobes; five or ten per cent more are mildly bigoted in the same direction. At least forty per cent express prejudice against the Negro." [7] According to Kenneth Clark, prejudice may be found in children at the tender age of three and is intensified as they grow older, becoming similar to the prevailing attitudes held by the average American adult. [8]

The Roots of Prejudice

Less than fifty years ago, some students of the problem maintained that racial prejudice is inborn and instinctive. Recent research has repudiated this earlier theory. It is now widely held that race prejudice is not inherited, but acquired or learned in the cultural and social environment. There is some truth in both claims. Prejudice, contrary to the dogmatic claims of contemporary social scientists that it is wholly derived from the social situation, is basically innate, due to the sinful pride and egoism of man. Race prejudice can be learned only because it has an "eager pupil in the inherently prideful and instinctively prejudiced will of man." [9] Prejudice, therefore, arises in the heart and is stimulated in the social setting. Myrdal is right when he calls the race issue "a problem in the heart of the American." [10]

Scientists have not sufficiently studied the psychological and social sources of prejudice to arrive at any absolute certitude about the matter. One theory is that prejudice comes from the desire for personal advantage, especially political, as is dramatically illustrated in men like Hitler and some American politicians who base their campaigns on racial supremacy.[11]

Another theory of the causative factor in race prejudice is that of ignorance. This is believed to be a factor because it usually accompanies prejudicial attitudes toward others. False beliefs about members of minority groups tend to take the form of stereotypes —exaggerations of certain physical traits and cultural characteristics of a few which are attributed to all. Two examples will illustrate this fact. The Negro stereotype is classified as the "lazy, happy-go-lucky, morally inferior" person, while the stereotype of the Jew is that of a person who is "shrewd, mercenary, aggressive, and ambitious." Such stereotypes are vague mental pictures which some persons have of individuals and apply to specific racial groups.

Fear of miscegenation is another source of tension and prejudice. People are frightened because they think that integration will encourage inter-racial marriages. No doubt intermarriage will increase with increasing contact between races. But this will be on a small scale. Thus far in the United States, where integration in the public schools has been in operation for a long time, there have been no indications of significant desire or compulsion toward intermarriage. In those states that have not forbidden miscegenation by law, the ratio of inter-racial marriage has been extremely low.[12] What the Negro desires most is not intermarriage but economic security.[13]

Finally, there is the prejudice which comes from the fear of economic competition. For many persons, the race question is in reality the problem of economic security and the threat involved in the ascendancy of another race. Hence the white man has sought to "keep the Negro in his place" because he fears the competition of Negro labor at a lower wage level than his own. A few generations ago this threat was greater than it is now. But now with minimum wage laws, the increase of job opportunities, skill, and competence, there has come an increase of resources for all.

The Functions of Prejudice

Prejudice operates in subtle and savage ways. One may have deep race prejudice and be unaware of it. There is the woman, for instance, who declared that she had no prejudice toward Negroes, insisting that she loved her Negro maid and gardener. She gave them good clothes the family no longer cared to wear. But she did not want her children to play with "colored" children. Moreover, she emphatically affirmed that if Negroes moved into the neighborhood her family would move out.

In a more dramatic fashion, prejudice is manifested toward the Negro in the courts of law, in segregation where racial groups are enclaved or culturally set apart in deteriorated areas of the community. Prejudice may also explode in terms of race riots in Detroit and New York as well as lynching mobs in Georgia and Mississippi.

The Price of Prejudice

It is impossible to count the cost of prejudice to the individual or to the nation. In terms of dilatory effects upon personality, the price of prejudice is inestimable. The segregator becomes calloused to human suffering or develops an inner "moral uneasiness" due to conflict between ideals and practice. The segregated tends to acquire a sense of humiliation, inferiority, resentment, frustration, fear, loss of initiative, and even self-hatred.[14]

At the national level, the financial cost of dual systems of education, recreation, and other public facilities creates a heavy burden for the taxpayer. Internationally the cost of prejudice in terms of prestige and confidence is high. News of discrimination and violence against minority groups and individuals is flashed around the world in a matter of minutes. The Communist press makes effective political propaganda out of every racial incident, leaving the impression that such occurrences are common throughout the United States.

Reducing Prejudice

Of all the prejudices peculiar to man, that of racial antipathy is the most difficult with which to cope. Perhaps the irrational element in this type of prejudice accounts for the critical nature of the problem. Hence, in attempting to curb this evil, it may be well to begin by stating the facts and fallacies about race.

Scientists, being more objective than laymen, have come to some realistic conclusions about the various aspects of race. Some of them are listed as follows: (1) all human beings have a common ancestry; this conviction is in keeping with the biblical and biological views of man, for "God hath made of one blood all nations of men"; (2) there are no "pure races"; (3) science does not support the fallacies of biological, intellectual, and cultural inferiority of any particular people, insisting that differences are due to social backgrounds; and (4) no evidence is available to show that race mixing produces bad physical results.[15]

Intercultural understanding is an important means of reducing prejudice. Intercultural education can begin in the home where children begin to observe differences between people. Here children quickly pick up from parents favorable and unfavorable comments about others. By expressing fair and favorable attitudes toward members of other races, parents can help their children develop similar attitudes.

Public schools can help promote racial understanding. Social studies provide a special opportunity for the teacher to introduce students to the facts about racial differences and ways of promoting good will. Actual contact with members of other racial groups can be had through the educational workshop.[16] Those participating must be carefully selected students and teachers from different racial groups. A schedule of activities, including presentation of factual materials regarding cultural issues and trips to areas where minority groups live, can then be planned. Exposure in actual interpersonal relationships usually results in a revelation of character and genuine understanding between all participants.

We are grateful for the findings of the scientists engaged in exposing the facts about race and how to reduce racial prejudice, tension, and conflict. But the problem involves more than accumulating facts and disseminating them through educational projects. It also involves the role of religion, and to this factor we now turn.

The Biblical Perspective of Racial Segregation

Since the Supreme Court's decision to desegregate the public schools, the Scriptures have been used both as a sanction for and against segregation. Some argue that segregation is not "un-Christian" and proceed to select passages from the Bible to support their position. Others take the same passages as a basis for integration. An analysis of these positions and passages may throw some light on the use and misuse of the Bible in the interpretation of Christian responsibility in race relations.

The segregationist takes the "mark of Cain" passage (Gen. 4:11–16), in which Cain is separated from the other branch of the human family, the "Seth line," as a general principle of segregation. The integrationist holds that this passage has nothing to do with segregation. Rather the "mark" placed on Cain was primarily one of protection, not separation. Besides, Cain and those from whom he was separated were blood brothers; thus separation had a religious, not a racial meaning. The separation was due to sin (Heb. 11:4; 1 John 3:12); and the counterpart of this separation is found in the New Testament in 2 Corinthians 6:14 where Paul counsels: "Be ye not unequally yoked together with unbelievers: for what fellowship hath righteousness with unrighteousness?" (KJV).

The "curse of Ham" passage (Gen. 9:24–27) is perhaps most

widely used by segregationists who allege that, in the curse, God doomed Ham and his descendants (Negroes) to perpetual servitude. This interpretation was also common in the ante-bellum slave days. Integrationists point out that the interpretation is based upon three fallacies: first, the curse is pronounced by Noah, not by God; second, the curse is pronounced upon Canaan and not Ham; and third, the descendants of Canaan were the Canaanites (Gen. 10:15–19), who were white tribes.

Another controversial passage is that dealing with the "confusion of tongues" at the Tower of Babel (Gen. 11:1–9). The segregationist contends that here God frustrated the mistaken efforts of godless men and brought about permanent segregation of all peoples on earth. The development of different languages was not merely natural or accidental, but has served the divine purpose as a means of preserving the separate existence of several racial groups. According to the integrationist, there is no hint that this was an effort at racial segregation. Rather, it was an attempt to build a center of unity and security for the people by their own power, without dependence upon God. The New Testament counterpart was Pentecost, where the Holy Spirit overcame the diversity of language so that all might hear the gospel. Besides, contends the integrationist, linguistic differences have no clear relation to racial differences. Witness the people of China living not more than fifty miles apart who speak different dialects not understandable to each other. Also note that the Semitic people themselves have a multiplicity of languages.

"Warnings against mixed marriages" (Deut. 7:3; Ezra 9 and 10) are used by the segregationist to support his position. It is noted that Ezra took steps to purge out the practice of intermarriage after the Exile. This action is supposed to emphasize the importance which was attached to racial purity by the leaders of the nation and their divine ruler. Integrationists hold that this restriction on intermarriage was not concerned with the maintaining of racial purity but to avoid assimilation with pagan peoples which would mean death to the true faith of Israel. In addition, intermarriages were allowed and were rather common between Israelites and non-Israelitic proselytes. Also, true Israel came to be thought of, not as a pure racial stock, but only as those within Israel who kept the faith (Gal. 3:7).

Turning to the New Testament, the segregationist notes that while Jesus loved the whole world, he did not ignore or denounce racial distinctions, nor did he advocate abolishing these distinctions. Did not Jesus send his disciples on their first gospel mission only "to the lost sheep of the house of Israel" (Matt. 10:5–6)? He carefully distinguished between the status of the two races before granting the request of the Syrophenician woman. The nonsegregationist declares that the Great Commission is to evangelize all people. Thus Jesus' dealing with the Syrophenician woman is clearly based upon religious and not racial differences. Too, the final Great Commission shows the temporary nature of the first mission to only the "lost sheep" of the house of Israel.

Likewise, Peter's "vision experience" is used by both the segregationist and nonsegregationist for support of their views (Acts 10:1–16). Segregationists rule that this experience merely marks the removal of Jewish prejudices, which had barred the entrance of the Gentiles from the household of faith, and sets the pattern for Christianity as the religion of all nations and peoples. Integrationists argue that thus to limit the meaning of this experience is to stop short of the account of Peter's visit to Cornelius as recorded in the book of Acts.

"Fixed bounds of time and habitation" (Acts 17:26) is another controversial passage. The segregationist holds that Paul here declares the unity of the race, but not the uniformity of believers in external relations. The integrationist declares that, despite minor differences, all men belong to the same human stock. And, since God "fixed the bounds of human habitation," it is evidently his will that the Negro share America with the whites.

Another controversial passage is that of Paul's statement about the "unity of all believers in Christ" (Eph. 4:3,13). Segregationists interpret this statement as a purely spiritual relationship resulting from mystical union with Christ. Integrationists give the passage a more comprehensive meaning, pointing out that Paul freely took Jewish converts into the Gentile Christian churches on the basis of faith and not race. Attention is called to the possibility that the apostle Paul was commissioned at Antioch by a group that contained a black man (Acts 13:1).

Finally, there is "the Church Triumphant" passage in which the segregationist sees a segregated church in heaven! (Rev. 4:1–6). G. T. Gillespie says of the symbolism of the rainbow that it

. . . accords well with the whole scheme of creation, providence and redemption to see in the rainbow which circled the throne a fitting symbol of the spectrum of redeemed humanity made up of the peoples of every nation, kindred, race, and language blended into a beautiful and harmonious unity, and yet each preserving its own distinctive genius and virtues, the better to show forth the infinite riches and diversity of the divine glory and grace throughout the ages to come.[17]

Integrationists take this interpretation to be ridiculous, contending that there is no indication whatever that there is any segregation of groups within that "multitude." And they reason that, if there is no segregation in the church in heaven, there is no valid reason for seeking to perpetuate this pattern in the church on earth.

We have examined arguments pro and con for segregation and integration based upon selected passages from the Bible. Obviously, none of the passages cited is specifically about race. For race, in the modern sense of the term, was no problem in the biblical world. Group antagonisms were based not upon race, but upon cultural and religious factors. Hence, the Bible has no specific teaching about "segregation" or "integration," as we know these problems today.

This does not mean, however, that the Bible has no relevance for the race issue in our time. While there are no "proof texts" for or against segregation and its attendant evil problems, there are ethical principles in the Bible which apply to every form of injustice. As we have seen, the principle of love to God and neighbor, as well as enemy, is the fundamental basis of Christian conduct. Involved in this kind of love is the principle of justice.

Indeed, justice is love in action. Biblical love is not sentimentality, but seeks justice for all. Love does no harm to, but seeks the good of neighbor in every realm of his existence.

The Role of the Church in the Reduction of Racial Tensions

Every major church conference in America has been forced to face the race issue. At these sessions, many of the denominational groups have gone on record commending the Supreme Court's decision to desegregate the public schools. Courageous pronouncements have been made about race prejudice being contrary to the will of God. Discrimination has been decried and the churches urged to work for the application of love, justice, and brotherhood among all races.

Pronouncements [18]

A few representative selections of comments on the Supreme Court's ruling in the school issue by major Protestant church groups will provide some notion as to their attitude toward this action.

From the Presbyterian, U. S., General Assembly, 1954:

The Assembly commends the principle of the decision and urges all members of our churches to consider thoughtfully and prayerfully the complete solution of the problem involved. It also urges all of our people to lend their assistance to those charged with the duty of implementing the decision, and to remember that appeals to racial prejudices will not help but hinder the accomplishment of this aim.

From the Southern Baptist Convention, 1954:

We recognize the fact that this Supreme Court decision is in harmony with the constitutional guarantee of equal freedom to all citizens, and with the Christian principles of equal justice and love for all men. We urge our people and all Christians to conduct themselves in this period of adjustment in the spirit of Christ; we pray that God may guide us in our thinking and our attitudes to the end that we may help and not hinder the progress of justice and brotherly love; [let us] exercise patience and good will in the discussions that must take place, and give a good testimony to the meaning of Christian faith and discipleship.

From the American Baptist Convention, 1956:

We recognize that during the past ten years great strides have been made in race relations in America and that it was a logical next step for the Supreme Court to declare . . . that our public schools must be integrated to assure equality of educational opportunity.

We fully support the Supreme Court decision and deplore the resistance to this decision in certain states where integration of public education has met organized opposition.

From the Methodist Church General Conference, 1956:

There must be no place in the Methodist Church for racial discrimination or enforced segregation. . . . The decisions of the Supreme Court of the United States relative to segregation make necessary far-reaching and often difficult community readjustments throughout the nation. We call upon our people to effect these adjustments in all good faith, with brotherliness and patience.

From the Augustana Evangelical Lutheran Church Synod, 1956:

. . . We urge our members to use their influence in the securing full rights of citizenship for all, and in discouraging any activity in their communities which would seek to circumvent orderly judicial procedure in the implementation of the Supreme Court decisions of segregation.

Practice

The above denominational pronouncements with reference to the Supreme Court's decision to desegregate the public schools are to be commended. It should be noted, however, that these pronouncements about integration of the public schools have not been translated effectively into action at the level of the local churches. A study made by the Presbyterian Church in the U. S. A. in 1957 to discover the extent to which racial integration had been achieved in the local churches showed that of 4,766 churches responding to a questionnaire, 3,964 were all white in membership or participation. By 1958, the number of Negro members in predominately white congregations was slightly more than 600,000 with about 375,000 in the Methodist Church alone.[20] Of the more than 30,000 Southern Baptist churches in 1958 there were only 14 with Negro members.[21]

Fortunately, among the leadership of American churches there is a growing consciousness of the meaning of the Christian faith for racial relations. A "creative minority" of ministers and laymen are facing reality with reference to the problem. This group of religious leaders see that a segregated church is not in keeping with the will of God, but impedes the cause of Christ both at home and on the mission field. And they know that it will be tragic for the churches in America if they remain the last strongholds of segregation.

The Minister and Race Tensions

The "key man" in leading the churches to act responsibly in race relations is the minister. To fulfil effectively this role, he must become intelligent about the race problem. This involves not only an academic knowledge of the problem, but also getting acquainted with individuals of minority groups in their local situations. He must discover how they live in the community and what their grievances and hopes really are. Then the minister can find creative ways of establishing better understanding between all members of the community.

People are more influenced by the minister's pattern of life than by his moral preachments. By being Christian in his own attitudes and actions in racial problems, the minister can influence his parishioners to be more Christian in theirs.

Further, the minister is a prophet of God, speaking his message to men. If he declares "the whole counsel of God," this will involve relating Christian principles to moral problems. For the Bible contains ethical teachings with implications for all the issues of life. The minister's emphasis should be primarily upon these moral principles rather than upon the solution of social problems for which he has little or no technical competency. In regard to race relations, for example, he can stress the biblical principles of the oneness of humanity (Acts 17:26), of unity in Christ (Gal. 3:28), of love to neighbor (Matt. 22:36–40), of the worth of the individual (Mark 8:36; Matt. 12:12), and of the impartiality of God concerning persons (Acts 10:34–35).

Relating these principles to the concrete problems of human relations will require courage, intelligence, and perhaps sacrifice on the part of the minister. Nevertheless, he must "speak the truth in love" and remember that it is often the fate of God's prophets to suffer for "righteousness' sake."

References

1. See Edmund D. Soper, *Racism, A World Issue* (New York: Abingdon Press, 1947).

2. G. Myrdal, *et al., An American Dilemma* (New York: Harper & Bros., 1944), p. xlvii.

3. *Ibid.,* p. 61.

4. *Annals of American Political and Social Science* (Philadelphia: March, 1956), Vol. 304, p. 44.

5. *The Citizen's Council,* a five-page leaflet published by the Association Citizen's Council, Winona, Mississippi.

6. Gordon Allport, *The Nature of Prejudice* (Cambridge: Addison-Wesley Publishing Co., 1954), p. 8.

7. "The Bigot in Our Midst," *Commonweal,* 40:582–586, 1954.

8. K. B. Clark, *Prejudice and Your Child* (Boston: The Beacon Press, 1955), p. 24.

9. Kyle Haselden, *The Racial Problem in Christian Perspective* (New York: Harper & Bros., 1959), p. 80.

10. Myrdal, *op. cit.,* p. xlvii.

11. A. M. Rose, *The Roots of Prejudice* (Paris: UNESCO, 1951), pp. 7 f.

12. John H. Burma, "Research Note on the Measurement of Interracial Marriage," *The American Journal of Sociology,* LVII (May, 1952), 587–589.

13. Myrdal, *op. cit.,* p. 61.

14. Arnold Rose, *Race Prejudice and Discrimination* (New York: A. Knopf, 1951), p. 324.

15. See George E. Simpson and J. Milton Yinger, *Racial and Cultural Minorities: An Analysis of Prejudice and Discrimination* (New York: Harper & Bros., 1953), pp. 55–64; Ruth Benedict and Gene Weltfish, *The Races of Mankind,* Public Affairs Pamphlet No. 85, 1946.

16. E. S. Bogardus, "The Intercultural Workshop and Social Distance," *Sociology and Social Research,* 32:798 ff., March–April, 1948.

17. G. T. Gillespie, "Defense of the Principle of Segregation," *The Presbyterian Outlook,* March, 1955, p. 8.

18. See "Race Relations—Denominational Pronouncements," Parts I–II, *Interracial News Service,* Vol. 30, January, February, 1959; and *The Christian Century,* February 5, 1958.

19. "Racial Integration in the Churches," *Social Progress,* September, 1958, pp. 27–28.

20. Liston Pope, *The Kingdom Beyond Caste* (New York: Friendship Press, 1957), p. 109.

21. Joseph Martin Dawson, "I Belong to a Southern Baptist Integrated Church," *The Christian Century,* November 12, 1958, p. 1303.

Recommended Reading

ALLPORT, GORDON, *The Nature of Prejudice.* Boston: Beacon Press, 1954.

CROOK, ROGER, *No South or North.* St. Louis: Bethany Press, 1959.

GALLAGHER, BUELL G., *Color and Conscience.* New York: Harper & Bros., 1946.

HASELDEN, KYLE, *The Racial Problem in Christian Perspective.* New York: Harper & Bros., 1959.

HAYS, BROOKS, *A Southern Moderate Speaks.* Chapel Hill: University of North Carolina Press, 1959.

MASTON, T. B., *Segregation and Desegregation: A Christian Approach.* New York: Macmillan Company, 1959.

———. *The Bible and Race.* Nashville: Broadman Press, 1959.

MYRDAL, GUNNAR, *An American Dilemma.* New York: Harper & Bros., 1944.

NELSON, W. S. (ed.), *The Christian Way in Race Relations.* New York: Harper & Bros., 1948.

POPE, LISTON, *The Kingdom Beyond Caste.* New York: Friendship Press, 1957.

Review and Expositor, Vol. LVI, No. 3, July, 1959. Entire issue devoted to "Church and Race Relations."

SIMPSON, GEORGE E., and YINGER, J. MILTON, *Racial and Cultural Minorities: An Analysis of Prejudice and Discrimination.* New York: Harper & Bros., 1958.

TILSON, EVERETT, *Segregation and the Bible.* New York: Abingdon Press, 1958.

XIV
Economic Life

The economic order is the process by which the material means for the satisfaction of man's needs are produced, distributed, and consumed. Its function is not only to provide goods to sustain life but also a sphere in which the Christian can glorify God and serve his fellow man.

The economic order is one of the most powerful forces in society for the molding of personality. An economic system leaves its stamp upon persons as well as products. Christianity, therefore, has the responsibility, in the light of love and justice, to challenge those features of the system which are detrimental to the fullest possible development of persons. This chapter seeks to set forth the biblical and historical attitudes of the church toward economic life. With this background, an analysis is made of the American economic situation. A statement is then made concerning the Christian doctrine of vocation and its relevance to the achievement of a more Christian economic system. Finally, an observation is made of the world economic problem and what the church can do about it.

The Biblical Perspective of Possessions

A Christian approach to economic life involves an examination of the biblical teaching concerning property and wealth. Here we find no "blueprint" for a Christian economic order, for neither the prophets nor Jesus were economic philosophers or planners. However, there do appear throughout the Scriptures ethical principles bearing upon eocnomic issues.

In the Old Testament the principles relating to property and its

144

uses are quite clear. All things, including property, belong to God. He created all things and therefore they rightly belong to him. "All these things my hand has made, and so all these things are mine, says the Lord" (Isa. 66:2). And the Psalmist declares: "The earth is the Lord's and the fulness thereof, the world and those who dwell therein" (Psalm 24:1). Property is a gift from God to be held in trust by men and used for human need (Lev. 19:9 ff.; Job 31:16–33; Isa. 58:7–8). Thus, ownership of property is not absolute. Rather, property ultimately belongs to God and is to be used for the common good. There is the principle of the protection of property owners against the aggrandizement of those who have the power to deprive them of houses and lands (Job 24:2–12; Isa. 5:8; Amos 5:11–12; Micah 2:1 f.; Jer. 22:13). The commandment, "You shall not steal," specifically demands respect for the possessions of others.

The above Old Testament principles concerning property are reflected in the teaching of Jesus. As we have noted, Jesus was not an economist, but basic principles, bearing on possessions, are derivable from his total message. For one thing, Jesus recognized the rightfulness of personal property in terms of food and clothing (Matt. 6:32; Mark 6:37). At least some of his disciples kept their houses after being called to discipleship (Mark 1:29; John 20:10). Mary and Martha kept their home, and Jesus loved to go there (John 11:1 ff.). Joseph of Arimathea was a wealthy disciple (Matt. 27:57). And Jesus appeared to accept the idea of land ownership and the relation between landlord and tenant (Matt. 21:33–41; Luke 20:9–16).

Jesus indicated that the property of others must be respected. He forbade theft and fraud (Mark 7:21). He attacked scribes "who devour widows' houses and for a pretense make long prayers" (Mark 12:40) and Pharisees who practiced extortion (Matt. 23:25). Thus, wealth gained by improper means is condemned. Restoration of ill-gotten gain is one evidence of true repentance (Luke 19:2–10). Beyond this, Jesus did not specifically condemn the process of acquiring wealth.

Absolute property rights were denied by Jesus. Man is a steward, holding all possessions in trust (Matt. 20:1–16; Luke

19:11–27). Property rights are, therefore, to be subordinated to human need (Matt. 25:40, 45). Economic forethought is a reasonable act but excessive thought for the morrow is deprecated (Luke 14:28–33; Matt. 6:24–34). This undue preoccupation with not only much wealth but also with modest material accessories of life is reproved.—"Therefore do not be anxious" (Matt. 6:25,31; Luke 12:22–29).

While Jesus did not condemn wealth as such, he did warn against its dangers and deceitfulness. Riches tend to choke the word of God, to render it unfruitful, and to dull one's concern for spiritual possibilities (Matt. 13:22). Earthly riches tend to create a false sense of security (Luke 12:16 f.) to keep men from the riches of the kingdom by a divided heart (Matt. 6:24). Undue concern for property leads men to make ridiculous excuses for rejecting God's overtures to the kingdom feast (Luke 14:19). It is no surprise, therefore, that Jesus declared, "it will be hard for a rich man to enter the kingdom of heaven" (Matt. 19:23).

Money may be spent, according to Jesus, in several ways. It may be used to meet the essential needs of the individual and his dependents (Matt. 7:11); to support religious institutions (Matt. 17:24; Mark 12:42; Luke 21:1–4); to aid the poor (Matt. 6:3; Luke 18:22); to pay taxes to support the government (Matt. 22:17; Mark 12:14; Luke 20:22); and perhaps he implies that money may legitimately be used as a beautiful witness of gratitude and love to Jesus (cf. Matt. 26:6–13; Mark 14:3–9; Luke 7:36–50; John 12:2–8).[1]

In the apostolic church, there emerged a *koinōnia,* a community of sharing of goods. We are told: "All who believed were together and had all things in common; and they sold their possessions and goods and distributed them to all, as any had need" (Acts 2:44–45; 4:32). It was a spontaneous and voluntary act of brotherly love in which there was a sharing of possessions on the basis of need. With the growth of the church, this pattern of economic practice proved to be impractical and was supplanted by the "poor fund." But this does reflect that for a brief period economic considerations were dominated by the spirit of love at a deeper level.

Paul the apostle did not specifically challenge the economic order or present an economic philosophy. However, he did provide some guiding principles for economic life. For one thing, he urged Christians to earn their living by honest work (Eph. 4:28). He rebuked idleness, declaring that, "If any one will not work, let him not eat" (2 Thess. 3:10). This statement appears in substance in the twelfth article of the U.S.S.R. constitution! Man is to work not only to support himself, but that he may have something to share with the needy (Eph. 4:8b). Paul himself worked with his own hands so as not to be a financial burden to the churches, though he had a right to their support (1 Thess. 2:9; 1 Cor. 9:9 f.).

Paul pointed out the danger involved in the desire to be rich, noting that "the love of money is the root of all evils" (1 Tim. 6:9–10). Men of wealth were charged "not to be haughty, nor to set their hopes on uncertain riches but on God who richly furnishes us with everything to enjoy" (1 Tim. 6:17).

No communist ideals appear in Paul's writings, but he did demand that those who had possessions share with others in "simplicity" and to distribute to the necessity of the saints (Rom. 12:8,13). As for his personal attitude toward money, Paul appeared to have had little concern for it (Phil. 4:11 f.). He made no pronouncements about the world of trade, commerce, and industry. These economic activities were beyond his ken and concern, for he saw the imminent end of the present world (1 Cor. 7:31; 11:32).

By way of summary, the basic principles of possessions in the Bible are: God created all things and all things belong to him; man is steward of all that God has given him to be used for human need; property rights are not absolute but secondary; possessions are to be acquired honestly and restitution must be made when wrongly appropriated; and riches must always be under the rule of God—otherwise, they prove to be deceitful and dangerous.

Thus there is no "Christian" economic system set forth in the Scriptures. Rather, we are presented with a few basic principles for guidance in economic activities. These ethical principles provide basic criteria by which to judge the justice of an economic order.

Christian Economic Concern Through the Centuries

In its long history, the church has expressed both radical and conservative attitudes toward the economic problem. In the patristic period of the church, some of the Fathers stressed the principle of communal property. An echo of the *koinōnia* in Acts is reflected in the institution of collective monastic life. But, for the most part, Christians "in the world" accepted the idea of private property, expressing economic responsibility in terms of philanthropy.

During the latter part of the medieval period, Thomas Aquinas, in his *Summa Theologica,* gave the clearest expression to economic concepts of that period. According to him, man has the right by natural law to private ownership of property which is to be used for the common good. He condemned usury, theft, robbery, cheating in business activities, and emphasized the theory of the "just price." Restitution he conceived to be imperative and charity the means of meeting the needs of the poor.[2]

The great reformers, Luther and Calvin, conceived the problem of economics to be basic to the Christian life. Luther insisted on the right to ownership of private property. Private property is necessary, he held, because of the fallen nature of man. Too, one must have something in order to give to others. Communism, he believed, is based on the exploitation of the capable and industrious by the lazy. However, he did not believe in absolute ownership, for the right to property depends upon its right use.

Luther attacked the practice of usury because the usurer collected his safe interest without effort or risk, contradicting the principle of the duty to work. Money lent on specified commodities must conform, he contended, to interest rates in keeping with reason and charity with four to six per cent per year as the limit.[3]

Luther had a deep concern for the poor and organized a "community chest" to work for their welfare and education. This program was to be supported by the church, the community, and the state. Thus, according to Karl Holl, Luther planted the first seed for the development of the welfare state.[4]

Calvin held that the right to private property is contingent on right use of it. But he saw that a fair interest is justified for the purposes of commerce. Yet he condemned moneylending as an occupation for the purpose of profit. To take interest from the poor, he held, is unjust. However, he permitted interest without restraint in case the transaction was with the rich! But where interest was justified and the magistrate set five per cent rate of interest, it was not, he maintained, always right to take that much.[5]

Neither Luther nor Calvin effected any radical changes in the economic structure. The capitalistic pattern of life was already far advanced in their time and, in the succeeding centuries, became the dominant economic mode of western Europe and America.

The rise of the Industrial Revolution in the nineteenth century brought unique changes in economic life. Mechanization of production spawned the new middle classes, new industries, cheap labor, slums, and exploitation. The classical economic theory of *laissez faire* gave great impetus to the development of the modern capitalistic system. Any controls the church may have had on the economic order were lost. Indeed, the biblical principles of possession were not only ignored, but reversed.

In the middle of the nineteenth century, English Christian socialists, under the leadership of Charles Kingsley, F. D. Maurice, Anglican clergymen, and J. M. Ludlow, a lawyer and fellow churchman, sought to meet economic evils by promoting trade unions, adult education, co-operatives, social insurance for the workers. While they were able to achieve some reforms, the basic evils of industrialism persisted.[6]

Roman Catholic thought on economic issues finds authoritative expression in the encyclicals of Popes Leo XIII and Pius XI. In a remarkable document, *Rerum Novarum,* May 15, 1891, Leo XIII urged labor reform, including the rights of the worker to organize, a minimum wage, a ceiling on the hours of work, and a protest against the exploitation of child labor.

Forty years later, Pius XI, in his encyclical *Quadragesimo Anno*, May 15, 1931, sought to defend charges that Leo's Natural Law theory of private property placed private ownership outside the sphere of the state and the Roman Church on the side of the wealthy class. He declared that the Roman Church had never denied the twofold aspect of ownership, individual and social. He noted, however, a double danger to be avoided: extreme individualism and extreme collectivism. Free competition and still more economic domination, he held, must be kept within just and definite limits and under control of public authority for the common good. Moreover, he recognized the right of state ownership of some enterprises to offset economic power monopolies which would threaten the common welfare of the people. He concluded that when civil authority adjusts ownership to meet the needs of the public good, it effectively prevents injustice and destruction.

To implement the Popes' injunctions, leaders of the Roman Church have developed an organization known as Catholic Action. It provides an instrument of social thought and action in the total social order. In economic matters, Catholic Action has been very effective, especially in creating an interest in the labor movement.

During the latter half of the nineteenth century in America, there emerged a movement known as the Social Gospel, which was a response to industrialism and its concomitant problems of urbanization, poverty, poor wages, slums, and unemployment. Its aim was not only the redemption of the individual but the reconstruction of society, including the economic order. Among its dynamic leaders were Washington Gladden, Francis Peabody, and Walter Rauschenbusch, all clergymen. Rauschenbusch became not only the intellectual leader but also the most satisfying interpreter of the movement. Central in his thinking was the kingdom of God which called for an economic system based upon the socialistic principles of co-operation, approximate equality, collective property rights, and democracy. By socialization of property he did not mean communism, but the nationalization of the major economic resources as forests, water power, minerals, and so forth. In his mind, the economic system must be brought into harmony with the ethics of love, personal worth, human solidarity which are the ethics of the kingdom of God. In practical terms, this meant a minimum wage scale, shorter working hours, better working conditions, public housing, social security, and numerous other measures later reflected in the New Deal program of Franklin D. Roosevelt.[7] While certain theological aspects of the Social Gospel have been called into question—its lack of realism concerning the doctrine of God, man, sin, and the optimistic possibility of the realization of the kingdom of God on earth—its concern for the transformation of the economic order in terms of Christian principles remains.

Contemporary discussion by Christian thinkers centers around the effort to find a tenable position between extreme individualism and extreme collectivism in economic life. The World Council of Churches, meeting in Amsterdam (1948), criticized both capitalism and communism for their ideological illusions. For instance, it pointed out the illusion of communism, which holds that, after the revolution, freedom will be established; and the illusion of capitalism, which holds that justice will be the by-product of free enterprise. The Council's official report concludes that Christian churches should "reject the ideologies of both communism and *laissez faire* capitalism, and should seek to draw men away from the false assumption that these extremes are the only alternatives . . . it is the responsibility of Christians to seek new, creative solutions which never allow either justice or freedom to destroy each other." [8]

At present, the National Council of Churches of Christ in America is sponsoring the publication of a series of studies in ethics and economic life, begun in 1949 by the Study Committee of the Federal Council of Churches. Already eight volumes have been published with others in preparation for publication.[9] Written by the leading economists and theologians, these volumes represent the most significant and comprehensive analysis of economics ever attempted by Protestants. The nature, function, and goals of economics are discussed along with the implications of Christian ethics for the economic life. In these volumes, the general consensus of the theologians is that there is no "Christian economic system" in the Bible; Christian love is the criterion of a just economic system; both classical capitalism and contemporary communism are to be rejected in favor of an alternative position between the two; and, a planned economy is essential for a more equitable distribution of the nation's wealth.

The American Capitalistic Economy

The American economy is generally described as a capitalistic system. More accurately speaking, it is a "capitalistic welfare state" because the system has undergone significant changes in the past few decades. Therefore it is quite different from the "classical capitalism" out of which it has developed.

The Rise of Capitalism

The roots of contemporary capitalism go back to at least the twelfth century. Capitalism was well advanced by the time of the Reformation, in spite of the fact that the Church condemned the practice of usury. Because John Calvin, the great reformer, recognized that a limited interest is justified for the purposes of commerce and emphasized the quest for wealth in terms of frugality, prudence, and honesty, he has been accused of being "the father" of modern capitalism. Max Weber, for instance, holds that the inculcation of the Calvinist creed elevated the quest of wealth to an ethic sanctioned by faith. Capitalism, therefore, is "the social counterpart of Calvinism." [10] Impelled by the new ethics laid upon it, the industrial middle class dislodged the ruling aristocracy, supplemented it with a bourgeois social order deep-sunk in materialism, and lost its original religious motivation. Now, claims Weber, a new religion is necessary to break down the old ethic before life can be "rationalized" so as to give a new *ethos* of economic justice and responsibility.[11] Obviously this is a one-sided view. Weber falls into the fallacy of "the cause" approach. By singling out one causative factor, he tends to neglect the fact that there were numerous others such as discoveries, inventions, expanding trade, commerce, and industrial growth which contributed to the rise of classical capitalism.

Classical capitalism may be defined as "a system of production for private profit regulated by the forces of demand and supply in the market." [12] Its philosophy is that of economic individualism as reflected in Adam Smith's *Wealth of Nations,* in which he claimed that each man following his own interests would be "led as by an invisible hand" to promote the greatest economic good for society.[13] Thus, *laissez faire* became the watchword for a good economic system. This natural law theory—natural wages, natural liberty, and work without artificial control—tended to become a divine law of economics.

Capitalism's method is competition; its motive is profits on investments; its end is the accumulation of wealth; and private property is basic. On the one hand, capitalism has resulted in vast capital (pooled capital acting under units of management in producing, buying, and selling) and on the other hand a vast labor organization (workers, bargaining power).

Cases for and against the classical or "free enterprise" capitalistic system have been argued interminably. It is held that capitalism subordinates the meeting of human needs to the economic advantages of those who have most power over its institutions; it produces serious inequalities; it fosters the spirit of materialism; and it subjects the people to such social catastrophes as mass unemployment during periodic depressions.

In spite of its weaknesses, however, capitalism has a strong case in its favor. Capitalism has increased productivity, brought about the highest standard of living in the world; it has sponsored philanthropic, scientific, and educational activities. Moreover, capitalism has been characterized by freedom of occupation, and has placed emphasis upon individual initiative.

Contemporary American Capitalism

Despite the merits of classical capitalism, it has not adequately met human need in our nation. Hence, the government has moved in to become the "governor" or stabilizer of our economy. As a result, there has emerged a modified capitalistic system called the "welfare state," in which private ownership is dominant. Movement toward socialistic goals began in the United States more than two decades ago with the "New Deal" under President

Franklin D. Roosevelt's administration. Under the "Fair Deal" government of President Truman, the nation moved nearer to these socialistic goals. The shift in party control in 1952 to the Republicans was not followed by a repudiation of the basic features of the New Deal. Rather, Republicans accepted and even extended some of its policies. Now the United States is committed, in principle, to the welfare state system.

Briefly, the "welfare state" is neither primarily socialistic nor communistic in nature. In the democratic welfare state, the basic freedoms of speech, assembly, and public action guaranteed in the Constitution are conserved. Hence, it is a "mixed economy" with "free enterprise" as a component of welfare. The state becomes the instrument of the politically organized community to promote the economic welfare of its citizens.

The welfare state stems from various efforts to alleviate by state control and action the major evil effects of the industrial system in America. It is characterized by numerous social policies such as progressive income taxes, social security, federal grants in aid, public housing, minimum wages, legislation for better working conditions, a bias toward the labor movement, a state and inheritance tax, and other measures designed to distribute the nation's wealth over a wider area. Few citizens in America would be willing to give up the social gains of the welfare state. Indeed, there is a tendency to further socialize the resources of the country.

There are dangers, however, in the welfare state. Among the problems which citizens inevitably face in such a state are governmental interference and control of economic, political, social, and cultural life; bureaucracy; difficulty of enforcing social legislation; and the tendency to shift personal responsibility to the state and to depend upon it as the dispenser of all the citizens' needs.

To meet these dangers, citizens must act responsibly in terms of Christian ideals. For, as Karl Mannheim has observed, only a generation which has been educated at the religious level will be capable of accepting the sacrifice which a properly planned democratic order must continually demand.[14]

Yet, the general consensus of leading economists and theologians in this country is that the thrust of economic development should be in the direction of goals characteristic of the welfare state. Professor Howard Bowen describes these goals.[15] He makes Christian love the over-arching goal and discusses eleven subordinate goals which are here summarized: (1) survival and physical well-being or access to the conditions necessary for health, safety, comfort, and reasonable longevity; (2) fellowship or satisfying human relations, and participation in political and economic decisions affecting the individual's welfare; (3) dignity and humility, or the opportunity to earn a position of self-respect in society without a passion for prestige or power to lord it over others; (4) enlightenment, or the opportunity to satisfy intellectual curiosity and to acquire skills of and knowledge for intelligent citizenship; (5) aesthetic enjoyment or the opportunity to enjoy and to appreciate aesthetic values in art, nature, ritual, and personal relations; (6) creativity in which the individual can express his personality through creative activities; (7) new experience which overcomes boredom through problem solving, new worlds to conquer, and new ideas to think about; (8) security, economic and social; (9) freedom to pursue one's goals without undue coercion and restraint, including ability to make choices and to think one's own thoughts; (10) justice or access to equal opportunities, regardless of class, color, creed, sex, or political opinion; and (11) personality, or the development of the kind of persons in keeping with the goals described above.

The Christian Doctrine of Vocation

Professor James H. Nichols has stated that the Protestant doctrine of "vocations in the world" became "the means of greatest penetration of Christianity into culture which history or faith has seen." [16] One means of achieving the above goals and a better economic life is through the recovery of the Christian doctrine of vocation. This doctrine roots in the biblical teaching, particularly in Paul's conception of "calling." Using this term and its cognates more than forty times in his epistles, Paul teaches that the Christian is called in three senses: first, to salvation; second, to service in the church; and third, to glorify God in one's work and station (See 1 Cor. 7:20 f.; Eph. 4:11; 1 Cor. 12:28; Rom. 12:6–8; and Philemon). Hence, the Christian calling is a calling to the Christian life, including the way a man makes his livelihood. But there developed in the early church the notion that those working outside of ecclesiastical circles were engaged in "secular work."

By A.D. 318, there emerged, as seen in Eusebius' *Demonstratio Evangelica,* a double standard of life, i.e., the life of those who would be perfect, to whom religion meant separation from all secular interests and employments, and the life of those who remained in the world and carried on the ordinary functions of human existence with a sort of second-grade piety.

A principal passage of Scripture used by the Roman Church to justify this dual morality was the story of the rich young ruler who kept the law but desired to be perfect. To achieve perfection, so the Roman Church taught, he had to sell all, take the vows of poverty, and follow Jesus. But obviously, in the case of the young ruler, Jesus was giving special advice, not applicable to all but only to an individual absorbed in his wealth.

Both Luther and Calvin sought to destroy this double standard of morality and to recover the biblical doctrine of vocation. Said Luther on vocation and daily life:

It has a great appearance before the world when a monk renounces all and goes into a cloister, and leads there a severe and hard life, fasts, watches, prays, etc. There is no lack of work; there is, however, a lack of command . . . therefore, it cannot be proved as a service to God. On the other hand it looks like a very small thing that a maid cooks in the house, cleans, sweeps, and does other housework, but because God's command is there, even for the small work must be praised as a service of God and it surpasses by far all the holiness and life of monks and nuns. For here there is no command of God, however, there God's command is fulfilled that one should honor father and mother, and should help in keeping house . . . And it is even very much so, what you do in your house, as if you have done it with the Lord God above in heaven. For it is pleasing to Him that we in our calling do here on earth according to His word and command, He counts it as if it were done in heaven for Him.[17]

With the rise of the Industrial Revolution, the Christian doctrine of vocation was largely lost in the increasing secularization of work. Daily work and divine vocation, long separated by the double standard, and bound together in Reformation theology, once again fell apart. Impersonal forces and the corroding touch of the modern economic system tended to depersonalize man and to rob him of creativity in his work. While the terms "vocation" and "calling" are still used, they have come to mean "little or nothing more than worldly activities pursued with diligence for their own sake, and for the sake of worldly rewards." [18]

With the increasing mechanization and impersonalization of our time, it is imperative that we recover the biblical idea of work and vocation. Significant efforts are being made in this direction. From the body of literature developing on the subject, one finds a growing consensus concerning the nature and meaning of Christian vocation.[19] A Christian vocation is one which renders a genuine service to humanity; one which meets a real need of society; a job over which one can pray; a job in harmony with love, justice, and human dignity; one which requires of the worker integrity, creativity, imagination, and social usefulness; and finally, it is one characterized by a sense of purpose.

Recovery of the Christian doctrine of vocation would contribute to the redirection of economic structures toward goals more in keeping with the Christian principles of love, justice, and equality. It is the task of the church, therefore, to clarify the concepts of work and vocation and to inspire men to act responsibly where economic decisions are being made.

The Economic Problem in World Perspective

Our country is an island of plenty in a world of poverty. Outside the United States, Canada, Western Europe, Great Britain, and a few other countries, poverty is the fate of millions. Yet the resources of the world are plentiful and we have the technological know-how to feed all the people.

It is ironical that many of the Asiatic and Middle Eastern countries and India, though rich in natural resources, have widespread poverty prevailing among the masses of the people. Lack of technical knowledge, communication, transportation, and a diversified economy make it impossible to produce adequate materials for consumption. Also landlordism, irresponsible businessmen and politicians, ill health, over-population, imperialism, colonial exploitation, and cartels deter economic progress.

The United Nations Technical Assistance program, Point IV of the United States, and the Colombo Plan of the British Commonwealth are constructive steps toward aiding undeveloped countries to get on their feet economically. Much more needs to be done along these lines. The alternative is to leave the way open to the Communists. The coming battle between Russia and the West will be an economic one. Unless positive economic aid and technical help is given to undeveloped countries, many of them will inevitably go over to the Communists who promise an immediate program of economic plenty for everyone.

But what can the church do? For one thing, she can preach and practice the Christian principle of sharing. Faith involves the sharing of goods with those in need. The apostle James declares that if a brother or sister is "ill-clad and in lack of daily food," it is sheer hypocrisy to say to them, "Go in peace, be warmed and filled," without giving them the things needed for the body (2:14–17). Besides the Church World Service of the National Council of the Churches of Christ in the U. S. A., there are numerous other organizations through which we can share our surplus goods with the world's needy people.

On her mission fields, the church can help to improve agricultural conditions, develop co-operative community projects as recreation centers, vocational and technical education, housing and health centers. As Eddy Asirvatham has pointedly declared: "If Communism is to be effectively checked, the church should take the initiative in combating idea by idea, plan by plan, program by program; and not idea by emotion, plan by platitude, and program by a vision in the sky." [20]

However, the basic motive of the church in aiding the needy people of the world should not be that of defeating Communist aggression. Rather, it should be the love of Christ which constrains the church to respond to neighbor needs wherever they appear. It is a tragedy that too often the church is spurred to action by some secular force rather than the spiritual force of love for humanity, robbed and left helpless on the highways of the world.

References

1. See Hugh Martin, *Christ and Money* (London: S.C.M. Press, 1928), pp. 43–44.

2. Thomas Aquinas, *Summa Theologica,* II, Question 66, Article 2; Article 7; Question 77, Articles 1–4; Question 78, Article 1.

3. Karl and Barbara Hertz and John H. Lichtblau (trans.), Karl Holl's *The Cultural Significance of the Reformation* (New York: Living Age Books, Meridian Books, Inc., 1959), p. 81.

4. *Ibid.,* pp. 92 f.

5. *Corpus Reformatorum.* Brunsvigae Apud, C. A. Schwestschke et Filum, 1882, X, 431; XL, 431; XXIV, 682; XXVIII, 121.

6. See Donald O. Wagner (ed.), *Social Reformers* (New York: Macmillan Co., 1934), Chapter XII.

7. See Walter Rauschenbusch, *Christianizing the Social Order* (New York: Macmillan Co.), 1912.

8. J. C. Bennett, *Man's Disorder and God's Design* (New York: Harper & Bros., n.d.), III, 193–195.

9. Published by Harper & Bros.: A. Dudley Ward (ed.), *Goals of Economic Life,* 1953; Kenneth E. Boulding, *The Organizational Revolution,* 1953; Howard R. Bowen, *Social Responsibilities of the Businessman,* 1953; Elizabeth E. Hoyt, *et. al., American Income and Its Use,* 1954; John C. Bennett, *et. al., Christian Values and Economic Life,* 1954; A. Dudley Ward, *The American Economy—Attitudes and Opinions,* 1955; Walter W. Wilcox, *Social Responsibility in Farm Leadership,* 1956; John A. Fitch, *Social Responsibilities of Organized Labor,* 1957.

10. Talcott Parsons (trans.), Max Weber's *The Protestant Ethic and the Spirit of Capitalism* (New York: Charles Scribner's Sons, 1930), p. 2.

11. *Ibid.,* pp. 27 f.

12. Eduard Heimann, "Comparative Economic System," *Goals of Economic Life,* ed. A. Dudley Ward (New York: Harper & Bros., 1953), pp. 126–127.

13. Adam Smith, *Wealth of Nations* (New York: The Modern Library, 1937), I, Book IV, Chapter II, 423.

14. Karl Mannheim, *Diagnosis of Our Time* (London: K. Paul, Trench, Trubner, and Co., 1943), p. 102.

15. John C. Bennett, *et. al., Christian Values and Economic Life,* "Goals of Economic Life" (New York: Harper & Bros., 1954), Chapter 4.

16. James Nichols, *Primer for Protestants* (New York: Association Press, 1947), p. 138.

17. *Sämtliche Schriften.* Halle: Herausgegeben von Johann Georg Walch, Druckts und Verlegts Joh., Justinus Gebauer, 1743, Dreizehenter Theil, col. 1962, No. 9, Line 16 ff.; col. 1966, No. 15, Line 9 ff.

18. Robert L. Calhoun, "Work and Vocation in Christian History," in John O. Nelson, ed. *Work and Vocation* (New York: Harper & Bros., 1954), p. 111.

19. For an excellent study of the meaning of vocation and a comprehensive bibliography on the problem, see John O. Nelson (ed.), *Work and Vocation* (New York: Harper & Bros., 1954).

20. "World Economic Problems," in *The Church and Social Responsibility,* ed. J. Richard Spann (New York: Abingdon Press, 1953), p. 156.

Recommended Reading

FLETCHER, JOSEPH F. (ed.), *Christianity and Property.* Philadelphia: Westminster Press, 1947.

MUELDER, WALTER G., *Religion and Economic Responsibility.* New York: Charles Scribner's Sons, 1953.

NELSON, JOHN O., Editor, *Work and Vocation: A Christian Discussion.* New York: Harper & Bros. 1954.

TAWNEY, R. H., *Religion and the Rise of Capitalism: A Historical Study.* New York: Penguin Books, Inc., 1947.

WARD, A. DUDLEY (ed.), *Goals of Economic Life.* New York: Harper & Bros., 1953.

WEBER, MAX, *The Protestant Ethic and the Spirit of Capitalism.* Translated by TALCOTT PARSONS. New York: Charles Scribner's Sons, 1930.

XV

Political Life

Christian ethical responsibility extends into the political realm. Some would deny this, contending that the Christian ethic applies only in personal relations. For instance, a leading political leader in a quasi-southern state declared that Christianity is "too sacred" to be injected into politics. But in every area of existence where personality is threatened or advanced, the Christian ethic is relevant and essential to its fullest development. Today, when the state tends to become absolute and to deny the basic freedoms of man, it is the duty of the Christian to participate in political decisions in terms of Christian principles.

The New Testament Attitude Toward the State

As in the case of the economic order, Jesus presents no political theory as such. Only incidental references to the political order appear in his teaching. However, Jesus' attitude and expressions do provide some guidance for Christians in political relations.

Jesus recognized the government and its legitimate functions in terms of maintaining order, collecting taxes, and adopting a monetary system (Matt. 17:24–25; 22:15–22; Mark 12:17). The Pharisees' question as to whether it was lawful to pay tribute (poll tax) to Caesar was designed to ensnare Jesus. If he had declared it unlawful, Jesus would have been arrested by Roman authorities. Had he stated that it was lawful he would have been looked upon as an unpatriotic Jew. But Jesus replied: "Render to Caesar the things that are Caesar's, and to God the things that are God's." H. D. A. Major declares that, in this answer, Jesus

161

"lays down the fundamental principles which must guide his disciples in those future crises in which human authority and divine authority—State and Church—make conflicting claims." [1]

Jesus severely criticized the evils committed by the government and political leaders. His strictures, it must be noted, were not directed at the government itself, but at the abuses of the government. Jesus called Herod a "fox" (Luke 13:32) and spoke of the leaven of Herod (Mark 8:15). He condemned power for power's sake, making it clear that the authority of the ruler comes from God (Mark 10:42–43; John 19:11). He urged the disciples to avoid the courts of law in settling disputes (Matt. 5:25). And he declined to become an earthly king, declaring that the kingdom of God is not of this world (Luke 22:24–27; John 6:15; 18:33–36).

Why did Jesus give such scanty teaching about the political order? The answer is that his main purpose was the redemption of persons, not the reconstruction of the government. But, as in the case of other great social issues, Jesus laid down the fundamental principles by which Christians are to be guided in political activities. Christians following these principles have greatly humanized laws and governments through the centuries of the church.

Paul's view of the state reflects an optimism which none of the other New Testament writers share. In Romans 13, he presents an adumbrated concept of the nature and function of the state and the Christian's responsibility to it. He sees the state as a God-given institution, functioning to protect the good and to restrain the evildoers. It has the power of life and death over its citizens, acting as God's servant and the agent of God's wrath against the evildoer. And, since the state is God's instrument to promote order and well-being, it is the consequent duty of all men to support it by being good citizens, paying taxes, and honoring those in power.

Being a Roman citizen, Paul appealed to his privileges as a citizen (Acts 16:37; 22:28; 25:1–27). At the same time, he recognized that the Christian's true citizenship is in heaven (Phil. 3:20). But just as the Roman colonists sought to fashion the life of a new colony after the model of Rome, so the Christian must seek to fashion the Christian community in accordance with the laws of heaven.

As did Jesus, Paul warned Christians against going to courts of law to settle their disputes (1 Cor. 6:1–7; cf. Matt. 5:40). Rather, he recommended the setting up of arbitration courts within the Christian community. According to C. H. Dodd, "Such courts, perfectly regular as private procedure under Roman law, formed the germ of the later ecclesiastical jurisdiction" in the church.[2]

It should be noted that the divine origin of the power of the state in Paul's thought does not mean uncritical obedience to any form of government. There is implicit in his teaching a divine limitation of the state; namely, that of the state's purpose to promote peace and justice. No doubt, he would have been more critical of the Roman government had it been engaged in an all-out persecution of the church. Hence, the general attitude of Paul and his contemporaries was that of submission to the state (1 Tim. 2:1–3; cf. 1 Peter 2:13–15).

Christians were soon to discover that the ruler could be a "terror" to the good as well as the evildoer. Refusal to worship the emperor as a symbol of the state brought widespread persecution and death to many Christians. Paul himself suffered death at the hands of the Roman government. As a result of persecution, the church developed an attitude of hostility to the state. Revelation 13 may be contrasted with Romans 13 to see the changed attitude of Christians toward the state. In the Revelation passage, the "beast" is the Roman Empire which promoted Caesar-worship and persecuted Christians who refused to burn incense to the Caesar.

By way of summary we can say that, with the exception of Revelation 13, the prevailing attitude of the New Testament writers toward the state is that of acceptance and submission. There is no hint, however, of absolute submission to any form of the state. Where the claims of Christ and Caesar conflicted, Christians declared that "We must obey God rather than men" (Acts 5:29).

In A.D. 313, Christianity became a "licensed cult" with the

Emperor Constantine as its patron and proselyte. Christianity became popular and persecution ceased. Christians actively engaged in political matters and served in the armies. Thus church and state were wedded, paving the way for the rise of medieval papacy's power over the Western world.

Is there any specific type of political order for which Christians should strive? What form of state appears to be most consistent with the biblical principles we have examined? To answer these questions, it is necessary to analyze the modern conceptions and forms of the state under which Christians live.

The State: Its Nature and Function

The state may be defined as a politically organized body of people, occupying a definite territory, being under a government free or relatively free from external control, and capable of securing obedience of its citizens. Among the conflicting theories as to the genesis of the state, there are three which appear to be basic: theocratic, naturalistic, and power.

The theocratic theory of the state's origin is the traditional Protestant view. Martin Luther conceived the state to be the result of the fall of man. Hence, it is not in original creation, but an order of preservation. Luther thought of the state as "the kingdom of sin" or "the kingdom of the left-hand of God." [3] The theocratic state found concrete expression in the city of Geneva and in the Puritan experiment of New England.

The naturalistic or Roman Catholic concept is that the state is grounded in human nature prior to the Fall. Heinrich A. Rommen declares: "So deeply is the state rooted in human nature that it would have grown also in the *status naturae purae,* i.e., without the Fall." [4] Thus the state in Roman Catholic thought is not a consequence of sin, but inherent in man's original nature.

The power theory of the state's origin holds that the state was established by certain groups which used it for their own selfish purposes. Karl Marx, for instance, held that the state is not a natural institution but a product of class struggle, a machine invented by the *bourgeoisie* for the oppression of the lower classes and the protection of privileged positions. Thus, in a classless society, the state will "wither away" to be replaced by a more just political order.[5]

As for the state's function, there are some basic disagreements among religious groups. According to the Roman Catholic Church, the state has both a protective and promotive function. Its protective functions involve, among other things, the maintaining of order, justice, protection of citizens from external danger, and fostering international interests. Beyond the promotion of the general welfare of the people, the government, and arts, the state is to promote and protect the "true" religion, namely, the Roman Catholic Church.[6]

While there is a lack of agreement among Protestants as to the functions of the state, a general consensus was expressed at the ecumenical conference in Oxford (1937) and echoed in the World Council of Churches meeting at Amsterdam (1948) and at Evanston (1954).

The Oxford Conference Report on Church and State recognized the state in its political sphere as the highest authority, but standing under the judgment of God, bound by his will, having the God-given aim of upholding the law, order, and ministering to the life of the people within it. The state, therefore, is not absolute, but the servant of justice. The Christian's ultimate authority is God. And while Christians are to render unto Caesar his things, it is God who declares what is Caesar's. Thus, where there are conflicting claims between the state and God, the Christian must obey God.

The primary duty of the church to the state is to be the church: namely, to witness for God, to preach his Word, to confess the faith, to teach its members to observe the divine commandments, and to serve the nation and the state by proclaiming the will of God as the supreme standard of life. From this responsibility, certain duties follow for the churches with reference to the state: that of prayer for the state; loyalty and obedience, except when contrary to God's will; co-operation with the state in promoting human welfare and justice; criticism of the state when it departs from the standard of justice; holding before men in their legislations and administrations the principles which uphold the dignity of man; and permeating public life with the spirit of Christ and training Christians toward this end.

With reference to the state in its relations to other states, the report declared that, as the church in its own sphere is a universal society, so the individual state is not itself the ultimate political unit, but a member of a family of nations with international relations and duties which the churches are to promote.

The state has a duty to provide the essential conditions for the church, including all religious bodies, to fulfil its functions to the fullest extent. Thus, the church should enjoy freedom to determine its faith and creed; freedom of worship, preaching and teaching; freedom from any imposition by the state of religious ceremonies and forms of worship; freedom to determine the nature of its government and the qualifications of its ministers and members, and, conversely, the freedom of the individual to join the church to which he feels called; freedom to control the education of its ministers, to give religious instruction to its youth, and to provide for adequate development of their religious life; freedom of Christian service and missionary activity, both home and foreign; freedom to co-operate with other churches; freedom to use such facilities, open to all citizens or associations, as will make possible the accomplishment of these ends, as, e.g., the ownership of property and the collection of funds.

The report concludes that, in the case of an established church, it also must enjoy the above freedoms. But if an established church is impaired by a lack of such freedom, it is the duty of its ministers and members to secure it even at the cost of disestablishment.[7]

Forms of the Modern State

Two major forms of the state in our time are the democratic and totalitarian. The latter form, which appears under the rubrics of Fascism, Nazism, and Communism, lays claim to man in his total being. It is a state, as J. H. Oldham says:

. . . which refuses to recognize the independence in their own sphere of religion, culture, education and the family; which seeks to impose on all its citizens a particular philosophy of life; and which sets out to create by means of all agencies of public information and education a particular type of man in accordance with its own understanding of the meaning and end of man's existence. A state which advances such claims declares itself to be not only a state but also a Church.[8]

In short, the totalitarian state is all-embracing, controlling not only the overt behavior of its subjects, but their thought-life as well. This is a costly type of existence for the individual and the people as a whole. The price paid is that of spiritual values, political and religious freedom, human dignity and freedom of enterprise. Brutality, concentration camps, fear, mass executions, false propaganda are characteristics of the totalitarian state. Hence, it is a form of state wholly incompatible with the Christian concept of life.

By way of contrast, the democratic nation is one "of the people, by the people, and for the people." By means of free elections, the people express their will and wishes through representatives in government. It is a government based upon the consent and participation of the people with constitutional protection for all citizens. A democratic society is characterized by more than one political party and provides the basic freedoms necessary for the preservation and promotion of human dignity and human welfare.

Democracy has its weaknesses. There is always the danger that certain minority groups may not share freely in the blessings a democratic society provides. In a democracy, too, many persons may try to get something for nothing while too few are willing to serve it. Wide indifference to participation in the selection of leaders and the formation of policies may prevail among the citizens. Freedom, religious and political, may be taken for granted. And the slow processes of democracy may appear inadequate vis-a-vis the totalitarian state. For instance, the latter can take short cuts to provide immediate social and technological assistance to countries it seeks to win. Also, it is able to mobilize its political and military might on a moment's notice.

Yet the democratic society appears to be more in harmony with the Christian ethic than other forms. Of course, democracy is not to be identified with Christianity as though they were one and the same. But the former, as we know it, largely derives from the evangelical Christian faith. Other forms of Christianity, as Roman Catholicism and Eastern Orthodoxy, have tended to oppose the democratic state. Professor James H. Nichols has rightly noted that the only forms of Christianity which have prepared the way for democracy have been associated primarily with Puritan Protestantism.[9]

Church-State Relations

Four contemporary patterns of church-state relations are in evidence. These are the Roman Catholic view of the church *above* the state as seen in Spain and some Latin American countries; the church *below* the state as in the U.S.S.R. and her satellites, where the churches are domesticated for use by the government; the church in *alliance* with the state, as seen in the established Anglican communion in England but with freedom for all other religious groups; and the church *side by side* the state in a free society with religious freedom for all religious groups. Of these four patterns, the latter has been achieved for the first time in the United States. Hence, it may be properly called "a new experiment" in the history of church-state relations.

A great jurist has called complete separation of church and state in the United States "the greatest achievement ever made in the cause of human progress." [10]

Contributing factors, according to Leo Pfeffer, noted lawyer and historian, were both practical and ideological.[11]

On the practical side are to be listed the English Act of Toleration in 1689; the multiplicity of religious groups in the colonies; the large number of unchurched people; the colonies developed for commercial purposes which manifested a larger degree of toleration; the Revolutionary War which tended to unify the population and to submerge internal differences.

Among the ideological forces in the achievement of religious liberty were the bold and successful experiments of William Penn and Roger Williams which influenced the constitutional fathers and religious leaders; the application of the social contract theory which had been popularized by John Locke; the

Great Awakening which broke with formal church religion and developed a resistance to coercion by established churches; and the principles of rationalism and deism expressing liberty, equality, fraternity, and an apathy toward institutionalized religion.

Among the major political leaders who urged religious freedom were Thomas Jefferson and James Madison. Jefferson's "Bill for Establishing Religious Freedom" was passed by the Assembly of Virginia in 1786. Later, in a letter to the Baptists of Danbury in 1802, Jefferson stated that there exists "a wall of separation between Church and State." [12] By this he meant that the machinery of the state and a church must not become meshed in such a fashion that each would become involved in the official functions of the other. Though opposed to an established church, Jefferson had a deep respect for religion. When he founded the University of Virginia, Jefferson provided a place for worship and a collection of religious books for the library. Also he gave his support to the proposal that religious denominations be invited to establish independent theological schools in the immediate neighborhood for the clerical professors to teach there. [13]

Among the religious groups which made the most significant contribution in achieving religious liberty in America were the Baptists. Historians are generally agreed that the Baptists were the most active of all the colonial religious bodies in the increasing struggle for religious freedom and separation. [14] William W. Sweet, noted Methodist church historian, has declared that Jefferson's part in the accomplishment was not so great as that of James Madison, nor were "the contributions of either or both as important as was that of the humble people called Baptists." [15]

Threats to the principle of separation of church and state in our country are clearly seen in the attitudes and actions of the Roman Catholics. For instance, efforts are being made to disparage the traditional interpretation of separation. J. M. O'Neill, [16] Catholic educator, argues that separation of church and state is baseless for "the wall of separation" is only a "metaphor" or a "spurious slogan." In his view, therefore, "an establishment of religion" in the constitution means an established church of any kind and does not rule out tax funds for all churches alike. Leo Pfeffer of the American Jewish Congress has offered such a devastating denial of this view that no reputable legal authority has since found an answer to him.[17]

Another threat from the Catholics to separation of church and state is seen in their demand for public funds to support their parochial schools. Already in some states bus transportation, textbooks, free lunches, and other "marginal benefits" are granted to Catholic schools. But, in the Everson Case (1947), the court held that "no tax in any amount, large or small can be levied to support any religious activities or institutions, whatever they may be called or whatever form they may adopt to teach or practice religion." [18] This decision effectively cut off hope of government aid for Roman Catholic institutions beyond the so-called "marginal benefits." However, the Roman Church will not be content with this small achievement and will continue to apply pressure for equal support as that of the public schools.

There is evidence which indicates that there is a threat to religious liberty in the Roman Catholic hope of changing the Constitution so as to gain support for its religion. At least Roman Catholic leaders are on record expressing such a possibility. Msg. John A. Ryan and Moorehouse F. X. Millar, have declared:

constitutions can be changed, and non-Catholic sects may decline to such a point that the political proscription of them may become feasible and expedient. What protection would they then have against a Catholic State? The latter could logically tolerate only such religious activities as were confined to members of the dissenting group. It could not permit them to carry on general propaganda nor accord their organization certain privileges that had formerly been extended to all religious corporations, for example, exemption from taxation.[19]

Elsewhere Ryan and Professor F. J. Boland of Notre Dame state that, should the Roman Catholic Church become the established church, non-Catholic worship "may" be tolerated by the state if "carried on within the family, or in such inconspicuous manner as to be an occasion neither of scandal nor of perversion to the faithful." [20] Both of the above statements have the official imprimature of a Cardinal and is in substance the same position of Pope Leo XIII.[21]

These and similar threats make it imperative that every effort be made to give active support to the preservation and promotion of religious liberty in America. Religious freedom in our country was not won without a fight and cannot be maintained without vigilance and aggressive action in its behalf.

The Problem of War and Peace

War is an ancient phenomenon and is one of the most crucial issues in the contemporary world. Today, Arnold Toynbee says, "war is the crucial question on which the destiny of our civilization hangs." [22] Another world conflict may spell the doom of humanity.

The frequency of war is startling. Pitirim A. Sorokin notes that there have been 967 major interstate wars in the history of the Western world from 500 B.C. to A.D. 1925. Thus, a war has occurred on an average of every two and one-half years during this period. Periods of peace as long as a quarter of a century have been exceedingly rare. [23]

With each generation the cost of war increases. The price of war in terms of human life is inestimable. In World War II, the United States lost almost one million men and about another quarter of a million in the Korean conflict. These figures, of course, do not include those millions of civilians maimed or killed in these wars.

In terms of money, war is waged at an enormous cost. According to the Defense Department, World War II cost $323,632,-501,000 and the Korean war cost $20,000,000,000. In this current "cold war" era, over forty billion dollars is allocated for defense purposes alone. By 1970, the budget for defense may exceed fifty or even soar to eighty billion dollars. [24]

Now we live under the threat of World War III which would be more devastating than all previous wars put together. The "just" war principle is no longer feasible, for no atomic war can be just in either intention or conduct. Paths to enduring peace must be sought if we are to survive. The new dimensions of war in terms of weapons of mass destruction make it imperative that the church take positive steps to achieve a permanent peace.

What can the church do beyond proclaiming the gospel of love, redemption, reconciliation, and peace? What are some of the concrete ways the church can contribute to peace?

One possibility is co-operation with organizations and movements as the United Nations which seek to establish peace in the world.

The church can insist on continuation of negotiations, no matter how fruitless this may appear on the surface. She can insist on continuous efforts to secure effective disarmament, international control of atomic weapons, and urge expansion of large-scale programs of mutual aid to undeveloped nations.

And the church can help to keep alive the hope of a warless world, envisioned by the prophet Isaiah, in which men will transform the weapons of destruction into instruments of human welfare. In that day, men shall "beat their swords into plowshares, and their spears into pruning hooks; nation shall not lift up sword against nation, neither shall they learn war any more" (Isa. 2:4).

The Christian as a Citizen

The Christian is a citizen of two worlds, the temporal and the eternal. As a citizen of the temporal world, he must act in the light of Christian truth in every area of his existence. This includes the political realm. Hence, his political decisions must be made in harmony with the Christian imperatives of love and justice. This is more easily said than done. Nevertheless, he must act responsibly in shaping the moral character of the society in which he lives.

It is the duty of the Christian in a democratic community to: (1) be intelligent, to understand the nature and processes of government; (2) participate in the selection of public officials and the formation of public policy; (3) work for the extension of justice, freedom, and equality to all citizens, regardless of race, color, or creed; (4) serve in places of political leadership for which one is qualified, regardless of the cost and criticism which may be forthcoming; (5) challenge and criticize any force in society which tends to deny basic human rights or to run counter to the claims of God; (6) align himself with a church and other constructive forces which seek to strengthen the spiritual and moral fiber of the individual and the nation.

References

1. H. D. A. Major, *et. al., The Mission and Message of Jesus* (New York: E. P. Dutton & Co., Inc., 1938), p. 148.

2. "The Ethics of the Pauline Epistles," *Evolution of Ethics,* ed. E. H. Sneath (New Haven: Yale University Press, 1927), p. 325.

3. *D. Martin Luther's Werke* (Weimar: Hermann Böhlou Nachfolger, 1915), XLII, 79 and LII, 26.

4. H. A. Rommen, *The State in Catholic Thought* (London: B. Herder Book Co., 1945), p. 228.

5. Karl Marx, *Communist Manifesto* (Chicago: Henry Regnery Co., 1950), pp. 11 f.

6. See "On Human Liberty," *Encyclical Letter Libertas Praestantissimum,* June 20, 1888, in Etienne Gilson, *The Church Speaks to the Modern World* (New York: Image Books, 1954), p. 71.

7. Section II, "Church and State," *The Messages and Decisions of Oxford on Church, Community and State* (New York: Universal Christian Council, n.d.), pp. 25–30.

8. J. H. Oldham, *Church, Community, and State: A World Issue* (London: S.C.M., 1936), pp. 9–10.

9. James H. Nichols, *Democracy and the Churches* (Philadelphia: Westminster Press, 1951), Chap. V.

10. David Dudley Field, "American Progress," in *Jurisprudence* (New York: Martin B. Brown, 1893), p. 6.

11. Leo Pfeffer, *Church, State, and Freedom* (Boston: Beacon Press, 1953), pp. 81–93.

12. Saul K. Padovor, *The Complete Jefferson* (New York: Duell, Sloan & Pierce, 1943), pp. 518–519.

13. Anson Stokes, *Church and State in the United States* (New York: Harper & Bros., 1950), I, 337.

14. Pfeffer, *op. cit.,* p. 90.

15. W. W. Sweet, *The Story of Religion in America* (New York: Harper & Bros., 1939), p. 279.

16. J. M. O'Neill, *Religion and Education Under the Constitution* (New York: Harper & Bros., 1949), pp. 42, 72, 82, 95.

17. "Church and State: Something Less Than Separation." *University of Chicago Law Review,* Vol. 19, No. 1, Autumn, 1951; see also Pfeffer, *op. cit.,* V.

18. Everson vs. Board of Education, 330 U. S. 1, 1947.
19. J. A. Ryan and M. F. X. Millar, *The State and the Church* (New York: Macmillan Co., 1922), p. 38.
20. J. A. Ryan and F. J. Boland, *Catholic Principles of Politics* (New York: Macmillan Co., 1940), p. 317.
21. "On Human Liberty," *op. cit.,* p. 71.
22. Arnold Toynbee, *War and Civilization* (New York: Macmillan Co., 1950), p. 12.
23. P. A. Sorokin, *Society, Culture, and Personality* (New York: Harper & Bros., 1947), pp. 496–497.
24. *Newsweek,* LIV, No. 24 (Dec. 14, 1959), 43.

Recommended Reading

BENNETT, JOHN C., *Christians and the State.* New York: Charles Scribner's Sons, 1958.

BUTTERFIELD, HERBERT, *Christianity, Diplomacy, and War.* New York: Abingdon Press, n.d.

CULLMANN, OSCAR, *The State in the New Testament.* New York: Charles Scribner's Sons, 1956.

DAWSON, JOSEPH M., *Separate Church and State Now.* New York: Richard R. Smith, 1948.

EHRENSTROM, NILS, *Christian Faith and the Modern State.* Chicago: Willett, Clark & Co., 1937.

KNUDSON, A. C., *The Philosophy of War and Peace.* New York: Abingdon Press, 1947.

LINDSAY, A. D., *Essentials of Democracy.* London: Oxford University Press, 1957.

MUEHL, WILLIAM, *Politics for Christians.* New York: Association Press, 1956.

PFEFFER, LEO, *Church, State, and Freedom.* Boston: Beacon Press, 1953.

STOKES, ANSON, *Church and State in the United States.* 3 vols. New York: Harper & Bros., 1950.

TEMPLE, WILLIAM, *Christianity and the State.* London: Macmillan Co., 1948.

VOORHIS, HORACE JEREMIAH, *The Christian in Politics.* New York: Association Press, 1951.

Index

Akiba, Rabbi, 114
Allport, Gordon, 7, 131
Aquinas, Thomas, vii, 148
Asirvatham, Eddy, 158
Augustine, vii, 8, 102, 112, 116

Bainton, Roland, 117
Bailey, D. S., 111
Barclay, William, 65
Barry, F. R., 87
Boland, F. J., 170
Bowen, Howard, 155
Bowman, John W., 52
Bruce, W. S., 13
Brunner, Emil, viii, 3, 94, 107, 113
Bunyan, John, 108

Calvin, John, vii, 148, 149, 152, 156
Carver, W. O., 61, 92
Clark, Kenneth, 131
Clement of Alexander, vii
Constantine, 164
Cullmann, Oscar, 80

Dodd, C. H., 163

Eusebius, 156

Fromm, Eric, 7, 103

Genung, John F., 36
Gillespie, G. T., 138
Gladden, Washington, 150
Goethe, 43
Gore, Charles, 57, 59
Gregory VII, 118

Harkness, Georgia, 3
Harnack, Adolph, 44

Heim, Karl, 95
Henson, H. H., 46
Hillel, Rabbi, 64, 105, 114
Hitler, Adolf, 132
Holl, Karl, 149
Hoskyns, E. C., 105
Hunter, A. M., 89

Jefferson, Thomas, 169
Johnson, Paul, 103

Keyser, L. S., 3, 10
Kingsley, Charles, 149
Klausner, Joseph, 43, 93
Knudson, A. C., viii, 102

Landis, Judson and Mary, 119, 121
Leo XIII, 149, 170
Locke, John, 168
Lofthouse, W. F., 44
Ludlow, J. M., 149
Luther, Martin, 102, 104, 149, 156
    164

Mackay, John, 70
Madison, James, 169
Major, H. D. A., 161
Mannheim, Karl, 154
Manson, T. W., 44, 47, 87
Marshall, L. H., 6, 102
Maurice, F. D., 104, 149
Marx, Karl, 164
Melanchthon, Philip, vii
Millar, Morehouse, 170
Myrdal, Gunnar, 128, 132

Nichols, James H., 155, 168
Niebuhr, H. R., 104

Niebuhr, Reinhold, viii
Nygren, Anders, 102

Oldham, John, 108, 166
O'Neill, J. M., 169
Osborn, Andrew, 19

Peabody, Francis, 150
Penn, William, 168
Pfeffer, Leo, 168, 169
Piper, Otto, 117
Pius XI, 150

Ramsey, Paul, viii, 104
Rauschenbusch, Walter, vii, 108, 150
Robinson, H. W., 35
Rommen, Heinrich, 164
Roosevelt, Franklin D., 151, 154
Rowley, H. H., 13
Ryan, John A., 170

Shakespeare, 24
Schleiermacher, vii
Scott, C. A. A., 69, 101

Shammai, Rabbi, 114
Smith, Adam, 153
Smith, John, 129
Smith, J. M. P., 18
Snaith, Norman, 13
Sorokin, Pitirim A., 171
Summer, W. G., 120
Sweet, W. W., 169

Temple, William, 9
Thomas, George, viii
Thompson, E. T., 63, 65
Tolstoy, Leo, 103
Toynbee, Arnold, 33, 171
Trueblood, Elton, 117
Truman, Harry, 154

Weber, Max, 152
Wendt, H. H., 46
Wesley, John, 108
Williams, Roger, 168
Windisch, Hans, 50
Wright, C. J., 93